AMERICAN PRESIDENTS AND EDUCATION

MAURICE R. BERUBE

Contributions to the Study of Education, Number 46

GREENWOOD PRESS

New York • Westport, Connecticut • London

Library of Congress Cataloging-in-Publication Data

Berube, Maurice R.
    American presidents and education / Maurice R. Berube.
        p.   cm.—(Contributions to the study of education, ISSN
    0196–707X ; no. 46)
    Includes bibliographical references and index.
    ISBN 0–313–27848–2 (alk. paper)
    1. Education and state—United States.   2. Presidents—United
States—Views on education.   I. Title.   II. Series.
LC89.B45   1991
379.73—dc20   90–24709

British Library Cataloguing in Publication Data is available.

Library of Congress Catalog Card Number: 90–24709
ISBN: 0–313–27848–2
ISSN: 0196–707X

First published in 1991

Greenwood Press, 88 Post Road West, Westport, CT 06881
An imprint of Greenwood Publishing Group, Inc.

Printed in the United States of America

The paper used in this book complies with the
Permanent Paper Standard issued by the National
Information Standards Organization (Z39.48–1984).

10 9 8 7 6 5 4 3 2 1

AMERICAN
PRESIDENTS
AND
EDUCATION

Recent Titles in
Contributions to the Study of Education

Getting Down to Business: Baruch College in the City of New York, 1847–1987
Selma C. Berrol

The Democratic Tradition and the Evolution of Schooling in Norway
Val D. Rust

Diffusion of Innovations in English Language Teaching: The ELEC Effort in Japan,
1956–1968
Lynn Earl Henrichsen

Improving Educational Quality: A Global Perspective
David W. Chapman and Carol A. Carrier, editors

Rethinking the Curriculum: Toward an Integrated, Interdisciplinary College Education
Mary E. Clark and Sandra A. Wawrytko, editors

Study Abroad: The Experience of American Undergraduates
Jerry S. Carlson, Barbara B. Burn, John Useem, and David Yachimowicz

Between Understanding and Misunderstanding: Problems and Prospects for International
Cultural Exchange
Yasushi Sugiyama, editor

Southern Cities, Southern Schools: Public Education in the Urban South
David N. Plank and Rick Ginsberg, editors

Making Schools Work for Underachieving Minority Students: Next Steps for Research,
Policy, and Practice
Josie G. Bain and Joan L. Herman, editors

Foreign Teachers in China: Old Problems for a New Generation, 1979–1989
Edgar A. Porter

Effective Interventions: Applying Learning Theory to School Social Work
Evelyn Harris Ginsburg

Cognitive Education and Testing: A Methodological Approach
Eugene J. Meehan

For my wife, Anne Clarke Berube

Contents

Acknowledgments

I am much obliged to a number of people in the preparation of this study. Professors Dwight Allen, Jane Meeks and Raymond Strangways of Old Dominion University were helpful. Dwight Allen shared his manuscript on a national system of education, Jane Meeks furnished leads on the education of Southern blacks and Ray Strangways, on economics.

Others have contributed in myriad ways. Dr. Mary T. Piana has been a supportive friend and a wise counsel for over a decade. Librarians at Old Dominion University and Norfolk State University were exceptionally cooperative. Dawn Hall proved a patient and conscientious typist. Special thanks to my editors at Greenwood Press: Mildred Vasan, senior editor; Arlene Belzer, production editor; and Carol Lucas, copyeditor.

Finally, I want to express my gratitude to the twenty respondents to a purposeful sample mailed to fifty experts on educational policy on the question of a possible constitutional amendment on a right to education. These include: Dwight Allen, Professor of Educational Reform, Old Dominion University; Stanley Aronowitz, Professor of Sociology, City University of New York; Terrel H. Bell, Professor of Education, University of Utah and former U.S. Secretary of Education; Chester E. Finn, Jr., Professor of Educational Policy, Vanderbilt University, and former U.S. Assistant Secretary of Education; Susan Eagleton Fuhrman, Professor of Political Science, Rutgers University; Bernard Gifford, Professor of Education, University of California at Berkeley; Herbert Gintis, Professor of Education, University of Massachusetts at Amherst; Marilyn Gittell, Professor of Political Science, City University of New York; Nathan Glazer, Professor of Education and Sociology, Harvard University; Gerald Grant, Professor of Education, Syracuse University; Samuel Halperin, former U.S. Assistant Secretary of

Health, Education and Welfare; Harold Howe II, Lecturer at Harvard University and former U.S. Commissioner of Education; David Kapel, Dean, School of Education, University of New Orleans; David Kratwohl, Professor of Education, Syracuse University; Allan Odden, Professor of Education, University of Southern California; Diane Ravitch, Adjunct Professor of Education, Teachers College, Columbia University; Joel Spring, Professor of Education, University of Cincinnati; Michael Timpane, President, Teachers College, Columbia University; Charles Vert Willie, Professor of Education, Harvard University; and Frederick Wirt, Professor of Education, University of Illinois at Champaign/Urbana.

AMERICAN
PRESIDENTS
AND
EDUCATION

1

Education and the Presidency

The role of the president of the United States in education is changing. As the American economy became sophisticated, the demand for an educated work force increased. This transformation was most dramatic after World War II as America emerged as a dominant technological economic and world power.

Consequently, American presidents have become aware gradually of national and international pressures to shape educational policies for America. They have responded in varying fashion, some more education-minded than others. However, national concern with education has increasingly developed within presidential councils. Some presidents, such as Lyndon Johnson and Ronald Reagan, were at the center of large-scale educational reform. Others, such as Richard Nixon and George Bush, have mainly continued past policies. In general, there has been an unbroken chain of presidential interest growing in intensity since Franklin Delano Roosevelt.

In the early republic, the founding fathers stressed education mainly as a tool for citizenship. Having successfully gained independence through a revolution, they were especially concerned that democracy be preserved, and they perceived education as the best means to insure that democracy would prevail at home. In the nineteenth century, only during the Civil War was there a presidential recognition that education could be advanced for economic reasons. Presidential interest in education was periodic until World War II. With the rise of an economy increasingly dependent on new technology, American presidents were confronted with the need to develop a more educated work force.

This is a policy study. My aim is to analyze presidential involvement in education and the reasons for it and correlate it with an assessment of national educational outcomes. I shall examine presidential efforts in education that have been successful and also had considerable impact as well as some that were not so successful but had significance either ideologically or as forerunners of future policies. I hope that as a policy study it will have implications for future policy making.

THE ROLE OF THE PRESIDENT

A number of concepts are crucial to this study. First is the idea of a corporate presidency. By the twentieth century, as the nation became more complex, presidential decision making also became more complex. Rather than a model in which one man made policy alone, a corporate model evolved whereby a number of presidential aides shared in the decision making. Indeed, the prime example has been Ronald Reagan's education policy. In that instance, Secretary of Education Terrel Bell almost single-handedly reversed prior presidential education policy by convincing President Reagan to embark on a course of educational reform.

The other important concept is that of the rhetorical presidency. There have been basically three ways in which a president of the United States has influenced national educational policy. First, some have proposed federal programs to address national issues. Second, others have mainly used the office of the presidency as a rhetorical presidency or "bully pulpit" to advocate reforms undertaken by others, mainly the states. Third, some have both used the bully pulpit and established federal education programs.

The concept of a rhetorical president has been developed by a number of political scientists, most notably James W. Caesar of the University of Virginia. First enunciated by President Woodrow Wilson, the concept of the rhetorical presidency is that the president influences policy mainly through communications. He becomes the "teacher and preacher-in-chief." Through mass communications, the president uses his office to influence public opinion and, in turn, policy makers on the state and federal levels.

According to Caesar, the rhetorical president accomplishes this goal of setting policy guidelines in three major ways: inaugural addresses, State of the Union messages and speeches. Our early presidents frowned on such a role and refrained from using inaugural speeches or State of the Union messages as policy guidelines.[1] When presidential power was at an ebb, Wilson resorted to the rhetorical presidency. Theodore Roosevelt's version of presidential advocacy was the bully pulpit.[2] Educational scholars and journalists have preferred that phrase, although political scientists prefer rhetorical presidency. Both terms essentially convey the same idea.

The advent of television has given the concept of rhetorical presidency greater meaning. With the emergence of such powerful communicative tools as radio and television, the rhetorical presidency has been on the rise. In Theodore Roosevelt's and Woodrow Wilson's era, mass communications simply meant newspapers, which reached but a fraction of the American public that television does today. On this sense of rhetorical presidency or its offshoot of the bully pulpit, American presidents have been able to mold public opinion.

CONSTITUTIONAL CONSTRAINTS

The role of the president in education, therefore, has largely been determined by the economic transformation of American society. However, as national educational responsibilities grew, American presidents have been constrained by a constitutional framework that appears outdated. Prior to the twentieth century, education had scant national implications. In a largely agricultural and mercantile society, the decision by our founding fathers to leave education to the states seemed reasonable. However, with the rise of the Industrial Revolution and, later, the techological revolution, the nation's education needs were compounded.

Nevertheless, American presidents have attempted to mold policies within this framework. The result has been that national education policy in the twentieth century, for the most part, lacks a planned and consistent form, and this lack raises the question whether there is a need for a constitutional amendment establishing a national context for education.

Conventional wisdom holds that education holds a low presidential priority. This argument is based on a historical consensus regarding the U.S. Constitution. Our founding fathers' failure to mention education in the Constitution came to mean that, by default, education had become a state responsibility. In turn, states delegate much of that responsibility to localities. Most importantly, these constitutional constraints have limited—and, in many cases, inhibited—presidents in setting national education policy. Consequently, few American presidents have exercised distinctive and wide-ranging educational leadership.

This conventional wisdom has been most forcefully presented by Chester E. Finn, Jr. Finn has served as an education aide to Presidents Richard M. Nixon and Ronald Reagan. Finn summed up his experience in the Nixon administration in his 1977 book, *Education and the Presidency.* "Presidents seldom think about education. . . . As seen from the White House, education is a low-level concern. . . . Within the broad spectrum of domestic concerns, presidents naturally concentrate on issues where the federal role is dominant. . . . Education rarely falls within that number."[3]

Finn argued that presidents concentrate primarily on foreign policy and conclude that little can be done in education because of the limited federal role. Most importantly, he concluded that "presidents see scant political reward for spending time on education."[4] Finn misread the dynamics of Lyndon Johnson's Great Society, in which education figured prominently. Moreover, he was a poor predictor of the political value of education.

Not all scholars agree with Finn's interpretation. Some argue that there was a profound misunderstanding by the delegates at the Constitutional Convention. Scholars such as Benjamin D. Stickney, Lawrence R. Marcus and Americo D. Lapati contend that there was strong support among the delegates for a federal role in education. They point to such influential figures as Madison, Hamilton, Washington, Benjamin Rush, Noah Webster and Samuel Knox as wanting "the federal government to oversee a national system of education."[5] They argue that this role was indeed the intent of the makers of the Constitution.

Admittedly a minority view among education and constitutional scholars, this interpretation has strong evidence in its favor. The most plausible case has been made by Benjamin Stickney and Lawrence Marcus. They reason that the delegates did consider education to be a national responsibility, although no specific clause regarding education had been inserted in the Constitution. They point to James Madison's journal of the convention as evidence. Madison, often regarded as the leading spirit of the Constitution, recorded in his journal that the delegates understood education to be implied under the General Welfare Clause—Article 1, Section B. That article states "that congress has the power to provide for the general Welfare of the United States."[6] Consequently, according to Madison, the delegates felt no need to spell out further a national mandate for education.

However, confusion evidently set in after the convention. Madison's journal of the proceedings was not published until 1840—well after the convention. The founding fathers then interpreted the lack of a specific clause regarding education to mean, under Article 10, that it should become the province of the states.

Nevertheless, Madison's account was corroborated by Alexander Hamilton. In his *Report on Manufactures,* issued in 1791, Hamilton wrote that "there seems to be no room for doubt that whatever concerns the general interests of learning... all are within the sphere of the national councils."[7] Moreover, at the convention Jefferson and Madison endorsed constitutional amendments for a strong federal role, and Washington later argued for a national system of education.

There is also evidence regarding the creation of a national university. Charles C. Pickney, a delegate from South Carolina, proposed a resolution to establish a national university; Madison seconded the idea. However, Governor Morris from Pennsylvania successfully defeated that resolution on the grounds that this power was already implied in the Constitution.[8] Moreover, the first six presidents approved a national university, and four— Washington, Adams, Jefferson and Madison—recommended it to Congress.

Nevertheless, despite constitutional constraints, some presidents have exercised considerable educational leadership. In the past generation, Lyndon Johnson and Ronald Reagan sufficiently provided national direction in education to qualify them as "education presidents." Johnson, who coined the phrase, became an education president by design, whereas Ronald Reagan became one by accident.[9]

Lyndon Johnson (the son of a former schoolteacher, his mother) possessed an educational background. A former schoolteacher, he considered education to be the cornerstone of his Great Society programs.

Johnson was adamant about the place of education in his administration. He informed his aides, who were developing policy for a poverty program: "This is going to be an education program. We are going to eliminate poverty with education.... People are going to *learn* their way out of poverty."[10] Along with his vice-president, Hubert Humphrey, a former college professor, Johnson launched the greatest number of federal programs in education of all presidents. He engineered the first federal aid to education bill and innumerable education programs from preschool to graduate school. In the estimation of many educators, Johnson was the penultimate education president. He provided not only national direction but also resources and programs.

Johnson's Great Society was a response to an outside force—the civil rights movement—which reached its height in the 1960s. Consequently, the educational reform movement of the sixties, spurred by the civil rights movement and given direction by Johnson, focused on the poor, especially the black poor. This equity reform movement saw national programs directed toward the poor for two decades.

Ronald Reagan also qualified as an education president. Although that was not his intent, Reagan responded strongly to the exellence school reform movement of the 1980s that was launched formally by Secretary of Education Terrel Bell's publication *A Nation at Risk: The Imperative for Educational Reform.* Whereas Johnson launched federal education programs, Reagan saw fit to use his office as a bully pulpit to spur the states to educational reform.

The excellence reform movement sought to strengthen educational standards. It, too, was a response to outside societal forces—economic competition from abroad.

A POLITICAL ISSUE

By the mid-1980s, education had become a national political issue. In the 1984 campaign, polls indicated that the American public ranked education second only to unemployment as a campaign issue—higher than foreign policy or the pressing federal deficit.[11] In 1987, a Gallup Poll revealed that Americans overwhelmingly felt a need for national leadership in education. An average of three-quarters of the public desired a strong federal role on ten of eleven issues from promoting educational programs to providing leadership to states with "national problems in education."[12] In the 1988 presidential campaign, members of the League of Women Voters indicated that they perceived education to be "far out in front" of such campaign issues as health care, arms control and defense combined.[13] The 1988 campaign was a watershed in American education politics. For the first time, all presidential candidates were concerned with education. Moreover, this campaign also marked the first time that education had become a bipartisan issue.

There is more evidence of a public shift of opinion regarding the role of the president in education. A 1988 Gallup Poll commissioned by the *Los Angeles Times-Mirror* during the campaign showed that education was the fourth main issue on the minds of voters.[14]

The public has also shown support for a national framework for education, although on the surface it appears contradictory. On the one hand, the public's support for national testing for high school seniors has increased from 50 percent in 1958 to 73 percent in 1988.[15] In addition, the American public has similarly increased its approval for national tests to compare results among schools from 75 percent in 1970 to 81 percent in 1988.[16]

Most importantly, Americans seemingly approve of national achievement standards and goals. Seventy percent polled in 1989 favored national standards and goals, and 69 percent of the public in the same poll supported a national curriculum.[17] National standards, national testing and a national curriculum imply a national framework of education.

The nation's disapproval of the U.S. Department of Education has decreased substantially. In 1981, two years after the creation of the department, the public was largely in favor of dismantling the agency (49 percent, with 22 percent no opinion).[18] Six years later that figure was narrowed to 39 percent, with 24 percent no opinion.[19]

On the other hand, the call for national leadership is contradicted by polls indicating the American public's desire for more local control. These same Gallup Polls indicated that 57 percent of the American public in 1989 asked for more local influence.[20] Correspondingly, the desire for more federal influence dropped from 37 percent in 1987 to 26 percent in 1989.[21] These polls indicate that although the American public has a vague desire for some form of national direction, it still clings to a traditional veneration of local control.

The need for presidential leadership is not lost on the chief educational constituency—the unions representing 2.5 million teachers, the National Education Association (NEA) and the American Federation of Teachers (AFT), AFL-CIO. Both unions saw the need to cap their local state and national political activities by endorsing and campaigning for presidential candidates. The AFT, the smaller of the two unions with 600,000 members, first endorsed a presidential candidate in 1972. The NEA, with 1.8 million members, followed suit in 1976. To date, both unions have supported presidential candidates only from the Democratic party.

EDUCATION AND THE ECONOMY

What has happened between 1789 and 1990 to make education a crucial national responsibility? The economic scenario has changed dramatically. America went from an agricultural nation to a manufacturing nation, to a postindustrial nation, to a technological society. Beginning with the Industrial Revolution in the mid-nineteenth century, Americans needed more and more education to be able to accomplish their economic tasks.

The turning point for a national concern with education came after World War II. America emerged as an international economic and political power. Somewhat reluctantly, American presidents were confronted with the educational demands of a technological age.

Prior to the Civil War, the United States was, according to one economic historian, "in truth an 'undeveloped' country."[22] After the war, the Industrial Revolution made America a dominant and prosperous economic power. By 1890, the United States was the leading industrial nation in the world and surpassed Great Britain and Germany. However, early capitalism did not require a great deal of educational preparation for the work force.

The economic transformation was astonishing. From a colonial economy dependent on agriculture and shipping, America entered the manufacturing age, an entry hastened by the blockade in the War of 1812 and the demands of the Civil War. In 1860, the United States produced only 205 short tons of raw steel; by 1900 that figure was 11,227 short tons.[23] Cotton textile production quadrupled in that time span from 845,000 bales to 3,687,000 bales.[24] As factories grew rapidly, the index of manufacturing went from a low 17 in 1863 to 100 in 1900.[25] The number of workers in manufacturing in 1892 was two and a half times that in 1877.[26]

This transformation was accompanied by a concomitant rise in population, productivity and wealth. In 1870, the population was slightly under 40 million; by 1900 it was nearly 76 million.[27] The gross national product in adjusted dollars was $7.4 billion in 1869; by 1900 it was 18.7 billion.[28]

During this Gilded Age, the key industries were iron and steel, textiles, copper and a newly established railroad system that could transport goods. Technological advances included electricity, the telephone and telegraph.

Nevertheless, early American industrial capitalism did not yet require a highly educated work force. For the railroad and steel industries, for example, the demand was for unskilled and semiskilled labor. Although universal public schooling was well under way, there was only a minuscule rise in higher education.

In 1870, 57 percent of elementary school–age children attended school. In 1900, that figure was 71.9 percent.[29] Indeed, in 1870, only 2 percent of seventeen year olds graduated from high school; by 1900 that figure was but 6.4 percent.[30] Most importantly, only 1.1 percent of college-age youth attended college in 1870, and by 1890 that rose to only 2.3 percent (although it must be said the population had substantially increased, making that a larger figure).[31]

This nascent industrial system was primarily dependent on capital investment "from a vast network of banks," according to the economist John Kenneth Galbraith.[32] By World War II and the rise of a technological age, Galbraith perceived that the industrial system with advancing technology required "trained and educated manpower" as the "decisive factor in production."[33]

World War II proved an economic watershed. Industrial capitalism entered an advanced stage: technology. The question was no longer how much America could manufacture, but how sophisticated the product was. Advanced technology required a more educated work force. This fact confronted presidents concerned over national policy.

In large measure, the federal government was responsible for the new technology. Government defense subsidies during the war created new industries and increased productivity. Most importantly, this aid hastened many technological breakthroughs. Among these were atomic power, electronics, chemicals and the aerospace industries. For example, electronics catapulted from forty-ninth to fifth place in the industries of the nation.[34]

One example will best illustrate the new age of technology. In 1903, the first Ford motorcar was produced in an assembly line in a matter of months. Ordinary steels were used, and the time to plan and produce a car was minimal.

By 1964, technology made the process more complex. Mechanical engineering had made quantum leaps in development. The science of metallurgy was created, resulting in better steel. As a result, production of the Ford Mustang took two years. "Technology," John Kenneth Galbraith concluded of the Mustang process, "requires specialized manpower."[35]

Still, it was an affluent age. National productivity rose from an index of 48.9 in 1929 to 135.6 in 1969.[36] The gross national product rose from $18.7 billion in 1900, adjusted for inflation, to $930.3 billion in 1969 and $4 trillion 526 million in 1987.[37]

With technology came dramatic increases in education, especially higher education, the latter aided by federal government policies. For America's educators after World War II, the task was to convince political leaders of the rising levels of education that were needed. "Technological change created a need for an educated people," the educational historian Diane Ravitch concluded, "and educated people stimulated technological change."[38]

After World War II educational participation rose significantly. In 1950, in a population of over 150 million slightly over 83 percent of elementary school-age children were in school.[39] By 1988, from a population estimated at over 245 million, over 88 percent were in school.[40] In 1948, 52.6 percent in high school graduated from high school; by 1986 fully 73 percent did.[41]

These figures are even more dramatic for college-age students. Whereas in 1870 only 52,000 attended college, in 1900 almost .25 million did so.[42] In

1950 nearly 2.7 million students were in college.[43] By 1986, 54.8 percent of the cohort age attended college, totaling over 12.5 million students.[44]

One can perceive the development of presidents' awareness of the economic basis for education through their economic reports made after World War II. Recognizing the importance of a more complex economy, Congress enacted the Employment Act of 1946 with the aim to "declare a national policy on employment, production, and purchasing power, and for other purposes."[45]

Under the act, the president is instructed to submit to Congress within sixty days an economic report on the nation. In order to "assist and advise the President in the preparation of the Economic Report"[46] a Council of Economic Advisers would be provided to him. The council is comprised of three economists chosen by the president with Senate confirmation. In addition to assessing the economic state of the nation, the council is instructed "to develop and recommend to the President national economic policies."[47]

This landmark in national economic planning also serves as a gauge of presidential awareness of the link of education to the economy. The first report totaled 47 pages; that in 1990, 419 pages.

In his first report in 1947, President Harry S Truman viewed education primarily as a means of social mobility. Moreover, he perceived a connection between government programs and educational effectiveness. He concluded that "relatively small government expenditures for health and education yield high dividends."[48] By 1950, he had greater respect for education for economic well-being. "In such fields as resource development, education, health and social security," he declared, "government programs are essential elements of our economic strength."[49] Indeed, he made education his sixth legislative recommendation: to provide federal aid to elementary and secondary education as well as a "limited program of aid in support of higher education."[50]

By 1990, the link of education to the economy was made even stronger. President George Bush's Council of Economic Advisers was more cognizant of the requirements of a technological society. "The new jobs created by the economy," the advisers wrote, "increasingly require high levels of education."[51] The "building of human capital," they concluded, "requires improving the performance of the nation's elementary and secondary schools."[52] However, departing from Truman's (and the Democrats') philosophy of government spending, the Bush council believed that the task was "not to invest more money in education, but to invest more effectively."[53]

NOTES

1. James W. Caesar, "The Rhetorical Presidency Revisited," in *Modern Presidents and the Presidency,* ed. Marc Landry (Lexington, Mass.: Lexington Books, 1985), pp. 15-34.

2. George Kaplan, "Hail to a Chief or Two: The Indifferent Presidential Record in Education," *Phi Delta Kappan,* September 1984, p. 7.

3. Chester E. Finn, Jr., *Education and the Presidency* (Lexington, Mass.: Lexington Books, 1977), pp. 103-4.

4. Ibid., 104.

5. Benjamin D. Stickney and Lawrence R. Marcus, *The Great Education Debate: Washington and the Schools* (Springfield, Ill.: C.C. Thomas, 1984), p. 6.

6. Ibid.

7. Henry Cabot Lodge, ed., *The Works of Alexander Hamilton,* Vol. 4 (New York: G.P. Putnam and Sons, 1904), pp. 151-52.

8. James Madison, *Journal of the Federal Convention* (Freeport, N.Y.: Books for Libraries Press, 1970), p. 726.

9. Americo D. Lapati, *Education and the Federal Government* (New York: Mason/Charter, 1975), p. 48.

10. Kaplan, "Hail to a Chief or Two, p. 7.

11. Nelson F. Ashline, Thomas R. Pezzullo and Charles I. Norris, eds., *Education, Inequality and National Policy* (Lexington, Mass.: Lexington Books, 1976), p. xvii.

12. U.S. Department of Education, "Responses to Reports from the Schools," in *The Great School Debate,* ed. Beatrice and Ronald Gross (New York: Simon and Schuster, 1985), p. 392.

13. Alec M. Gallup and David Clark, "The 19th Annual Gallup Poll of the Public's Attitudes Toward the Public Schools," *Phi Delta Kappan,* September 1987, p. 23.

14. Edward B. Fiske, "How Education Came to Be a Campaign Issue," *New York Times* (Education Supplement), January 3, 1988, Sec. 12, p. 30.

15. *New York Times,* September 11, 1988, p. E-31.

16. Alec M. Gallup and Stanley M. Elam, "The 20th Annual Gallup Poll of the Public's Attitudes Toward the Public Schools," *Phi Delta Kappan,* September 1988, p. 41.

17. Ibid.

18. Stanley E. Elam and Alec M. Gallup, "The 21st Annual Gallup Poll of the Public's Attitudes Toward the Public Schools," *Phi Delta Kappan,* September 1989, p. 44.

19. Alec M. Gallup, "The 13th Annual Gallup Poll of the Public's Attitudes Toward the Public Schools," *Phi Delta Kappan,* September 1981, p. 46.

20. Gallup and Clark, "The 19th Annual Gallup Poll," p. 23.

21. *New York Times,* December 26, 1989, p. B-10.

22. Ibid.

23. Edward C. Kirkland, *Industry Comes of Age: Business, Labor, and Public Policy 1860-1897* (New York: Holt, Rinehart and Winston, 1961), p. 102.

24. U.S. Bureau of the Census, *Historical Statistics of the United States: Colonial Times to 1970, Part Two* (Washington, D.C.: U.S. Government Printing Office, September 1975), p. 693.

25. Ibid., p. 689.

26. Ibid., p. 667.

27. Ray Ginger, *Age of Excess: The United States from 1877 to 1914* (New York: Macmillan, 1975), p. 40.

28. U.S. Bureau of the Census, *Historical Statistics of the United States: Colonial*

Times to 1970, Part One (Washington, D.C.: U.S. Government Printing Office, September 1975), p. 8.

29. Ibid., p. 224; U.S. Department of Commerce, *Statistical Abstract of the United States* (Washington, D.C.: U.S. Government Printing Office, January 1989), p. 421.

30. National Center for Educational Statistics, *Digest of Educational Statistics, 1989* (Washington, D.C.: U.S. Government Printing Office, December 1989), p. 45.

31. Ibid., p. 103.

32. Page Smith, *The Rise of Industrial America: A People's History of the Post Reconstruction Era,* vol. 6 (New York: McGraw-Hill, 1984), p. 590.

33. John Kenneth Galbraith, *The New Industrial State* (Boston: Houghton Mifflin, 1967), p. 282.

34. Ibid., p. 370.

35. William H. Chafe, *The Unfinished Journey: America Since World War II* (New York: Oxford University Press, 1986), p. 113.

36. Galbraith, *The New Industrial State,* p. 15.

37. U.S. Department of Census, *Historical Statistics of the United States, Part Two,* p. 948.

38. Ibid., p. 224; U.S. Department of Commerce, *Statistical Abstract of the United States,* p. 421.

39. Diane Ravitch, *The Troubled Crusade: American Education 1945-1980* (New York: Basic Books, 1983), p. 10.

40. National Center for Educational Statistics, *Digest of Educational Statistics,* p. 45; U.S. Department of Commerce, *Statistical Abstract of the United States* (Washington, D.C.: Government Printing Office, January 1989).

41. U.S. Department of Commerce, *Statistical Abstract of the United States,* p. 7.

42. Ibid.

43. National Center for Educational Statistics, *Digest of Educational Statistics,* p. 103.

44. Ibid., p. 106.

45. U.S. Department of Commerce, *Statistical Abstract of the United States,* p. 147.

46. *The Economic Reports of the President: January, 1948, January, 1947, July, 1947* (New York: Reynal and Hitchcock, 1948), p. 167.

47. Ibid., p. 169.

48. Ibid.

49. Ibid., p. 63.

50. *The Economic Reports of the President, 1950-1952* (Washington, D.C.: U.S. Government Printing Office, 1952), p. 8.

51. Ibid., p. 16.

52. *Economic Report of the President 1990* (Washington, D.C.: U.S. Government Printing Office, February 1990), pp. 26-27.

53. Ibid., p. 27.

2

Education for Democracy

In the early years of the republic through the nineteenth century and into the twentieth century, presidential interest in education was periodic. Initially, this interest focused on education for citizenship. With the exception of Lincoln's signing the Morrill Land Grant Act, which helped shore up agriculture, there was little economic base to presidential interest in education. Only with Woodrow Wilson in the early twentieth century was there the beginning of an awareness of the need for education in an industrial state.

This slowly developing presidential recognition of an economic matrix for education paralleled the economic devleopment of America. Colonial America was primarily dependent on shipping. Agriculture and the beginnings of industry marked a prosperous first half of the nineteenth century. The Civil War witnessed the birth of the Industrial Revolution, which brought more prosperity in the second half of the nineteenth century as heavy industry flourished. Nascent capitalism in the late nineteenth and early twentieth centuries was still basically rough hewn, with little need for a highly educated work force.

For the founding fathers, education was vital as a means to groom citizens for the new democracy. Benjamin Rush—physician and signer of the Declaration of Independence—considered the prime task of the new republic to be no less than to form a "national character" whereby "a true Republican cherishes no passion but a love for liberty."[1] In this spirit, he wrote a letter in 1787 "to the citizens of Philadelphia," published in the *Independent Gazetteer*, urging free schools for the "children of the poor."[2] His main concern—echoed by many of his collegues—was that "an uneducated citizenry could undermine the new democracy." He wrote, "In short, where the common people are ignorant and vicious "a nation, and above all a republican nation, can never be long free and happy."[3]

This sentiment was shared by the author of the Declaration of Independence, Thomas Jefferson. In his 1779 "Bill for the More General Diffusion of Knowledge" in his native state of Virginia, Jefferson proposed a public school system whose aim was education for democracy. "It is believed," he wrote, "that the most effectual means of preventing (tyranny) would be, to illuminate, as far as practicable, the minds of the people at large."[4]

In his 1796 Farewell Address, President George Washington (1789-1797) urged the new national government to "promote then as an object of primary importance, Institutions for the general diffusion of knowledge."[5] Washington's purpose was to promote democracy. "In proportion as the structure of government gives force to public opinion," he declared, "it is essential that public opinion be enlightened."[6]

James Madison (1809-1817) reinforced the need to educate for democracy. In a letter to a friend, he distilled his sentiments on the matter:

Learned institutions ought to be favorite objects with every free people. They throw that light over the public mind which is the best security against crafty and dangerous encroachments on the public liberty.... The American people owe it to themselves, and to the cause of Free Government, to prove by their establishments for the advancement and diffusion of knowledge.... What spectacle can be more edifying or more seasonable than that of Liberty and Learning, each leaning on the other for their mutual and surest support.[7]

A NATIONAL FOCUS

The first periodic presidential interest in education developed in the early days of the republic. Some educational reformers argued for a national system of education. The first six presidents—Washington, Adams, Jefferson, Madison, Monroe and Quincy Adams—favored a national university, while most of the founding fathers favored a state system of education. This first surge in presidential interest in education lasted from the birth of the republic.

There was some sentiment for a national system of education. In 1795, the American Philosophical Society established an essay contest. Seven areas were to be explored in essays, mostly on practical matters, including the best methods of preserving peaches, improving ship pumps, constructing lamps and such. One area was more philosophical in nature: how to develop the best "system of liberal education ... best calculated to promote the general welfare of the United States ... [with] a plan for instituting and conducting schools in this country."[8]

Two young colonial intellectuals won the essay contest on a national school system: Rev. Samuel Knox and Samuel Harrison Smith. Knox had been born in Ireland and had immigrated to the United States a year prior to winning the contest at age twenty-nine. He had been educated at the University of Glasgow in Scotland and went on to head a school in America. Smith was the youngest of the essayists at age twenty-four and had graduated from the University of Pennsylvania at age fifteen. He went on to become a journalist and editor of the *National Intelligence*, the official organ of the Jeffersonians.

In their arguments for a national system of education, the two young essayists constructed similar scenarios. They advocated a national system of public education at the local, state and federal levels, the latter involvement being a national university. Moreover, they both proposed national boards of education to oversee this sytstem with broad powers over curriculum. (A similar proposal was made in 1990 by Dwight Allen of Old Dominion University; see chapter 7.)

Knox presented the more elaborate essay. In approxmately one hundred book pages, Knox outlined his plan for a national system. For him, "the importance of establishing a system of national education" was paramount.[9] He proposed a system of "parish schools in each county of every state," country schools, state colleges and a national university.[10]

Knox advocated a national board of education to manage this system and to "preside over the general interests of literary instruction, to digest, direct and arrange an uniform system."[11] This board would be comprised of one or two "gentlemen" to be appointed by their respective state governments.

According to Knox, the prime reason for such a national system was the need for a common core of learning in the new republic so as to avoid that "diversity of modes of instruction...(which) tend not only to confound and obstruct...but also give occasion to many other inconveniences and disagreeable consequences."[12]

Although considerably briefer, Smith's proposals were remarkably similar. Smith argued that "it is the duty of a nation to superintend and even to coerce the education of children."[13] He recommended that "every male child" be educated in public schools between the ages of five and eighteen in a system comprised of "primary schools, of colleges and of a *University*."[14] His national university would be composed of students "promoted from the colleges."[15] Smith charged his national board of education "to form a system of national education to be observed in the university, the colleges and the primary schools."[16] His board would differ from that of Knox in that it would consist of fourteen educators representing areas of learning from languages to sciences.

More plausible was the call for a national university. The first six presidents suggested to Congress that such a university might be desirable; however, underlying that controversy was the dubious constitutionality of the issue. Some like Jefferson went one step further and proposed a constitutional amendment. There were many calls for a wide range of constitutional amendments in the formation of the new republic—all but two of which were rejected by Congress before the Civil War. Consequently, the involvement of these presidents did not go much beyond the suggestion stage.

The sentiment for a national university originated at the Constitutional Convention in 1787. James Madison and Charles Pickney proposed that the convention "establish a university, in which no preferences or distinctions should be allowed because of religion."[17] The delegates refused to do so by a vote of seven to four. However, some confusion ensued, leaving a minority, such as Madison, believing that the federal right to establish a university was implied in the general welfare clause of the Constitution.

The campaign for a national university was to last two decades. In 1788, Benjamin Rush published another letter "to friends of the federal government" urging that "one of the first acts of the new Congress be, to establish within the district to be allotted to them, a federal university, into which the youth of the United States shall be received after they finish their studies."[18] Moreover, he proposed that only graduates of this university be eligible for federal service. Rush believed that a federal university "will begin the golden age of the United States."[19]

In 1790, President Washington sent a request to Congress for a national university with an implied suggestion that he would endow the institution himself. In his message, Washington argued that a national university would insure democracy at home. According to Washington, a national university would contribute "to the security of a free Constitution in various ways," not the least being "by teaching the people themselves to know and to value their own rights."[20]

President Madison's (1809-1817) message to Congress reiterated the theme of education for democracy. Madison comented that "while it is universally admitted that a well instructed people alone can be permanently a free people...I cannot presume it to be unreasonable to invite your attention to the advantages of super-adding to the means of education... a seminary of learning, instituted by the National Legislature."[21] For Madison one benefit would be "expanding patriotism" so that "the features of national character will be multiplied."[22]

Madison suggested a national university to Congress in four annual messages. How the last was received in 1816 indicates the lack of strong presidential pressure to pursue the matter because of the unconstitutional overtones to the project.

In December 1816, Richard H. Wilde of Georgia was selected in the House of Representatives to head a committee to follow up the president's suggestion. Wilde's committee drew up a bill for the establishment of a national university and reported to Congress in December 1916. At this juncture, Wilde recommended in strong language that the president's idea be pursued. He chided his fellow legislators that they would be subject to a "censure more serious than that of merely neglecting the successive recommendations of several Chief magistrates" should they ignore Madison's request.[23] Moreover, Wilde argued that a national university was "an object admitted by most persons to be desirable, and by many believed to be both practical and expedient."[24] The time seemed ripe due to the "prosperous state of our finances leaving a large unappropriated surplus."[25]

The Wilde committee recommended a bill that would allocate large powers to the president. Section 3 gave the president the major responsibility of preparing a "plan for the regulation and government of said university."[26]

Before the Wilde bill came to the floor for discussion, the issue of constitutionality arose. Congressman Atherton from New Hampshire offered a constitutional amendment to permit the creation of a national university. Atherton's resolution read as follows: "The Congress shall have power to establish a national university."[27] Without debate, Atherton's resolution was defeated by a vote of eighty-six to fifty-four.

President Madison's decision not to marshal his forces on the issue stung Wilde. He bitterly informed the House that he had had: "the misfortune ... to be appointed the chairman of a select committee to whom was referred a very small and a very unimportant portion of the President's message."[28]

Nevertheless, Wilde had a "very strong conviction that [the bill] would succeed" and that "certainly it ought."[29] However, the unwillingness of the House and the lack of presidential support persuaded him to revise his opinion. Consequently, he notified his colleagues in sarcastic language that it was "high time that [a national university] should be interred—not with obituary honors, of which it was no wise worthy—but with the bare common decencies of Christian burial."[30] He moved that "the bill for establishing a National University ... be indefinitely postponed."[31]

THOMAS JEFFERSON (1801–1809): THE FIRST EDUCATION PRESIDENT

Thomas Jefferson was, perhaps, the most educationally minded of the founding fathers. He saw education as a tool for democracy and urged many educational reforms; however, as president his interest in education was muted from fear of the constitutional issue. He submitted to Congress a recommendation for a constitutional amendment to provide for some national direction but, according to his biographers, did not pursue the issue. His main credentials as an education president rest with his efforts outside the presidential office.

A scholar, architect, linguist and an archaeologist, Jefferson epitomized the new man of the Enlightenment. Indeed, Jefferson described his affinity for learning as a "canine appetite for knowledge."[32] Most importantly, Jefferson distilled his philosophy of education: "Well, directed education improves the morals, enlarges the minds, enlightens the councils, instructs the industry, and advances the power, the prosperity, and the happiness of the nation."[33]

Jefferson's emphasis on education was well ahead of his time, and his plan for schooling in his native state of Virginia was radical for its day. He proposed that both boys and girls attend schools. Jefferson's plan "for the more general diffusion of knowledge" has been called by modern scholars "the most seminal proposal in the history of American public education."[34]

The Jefferson proposal called for a "hundred schools" that students could attend for the first three years at no cost. At the next level would be grammar schools at the ratio of one to every ten of the "hundred schools." In the grammar school tuition and board could be required but a limited number of scholarships would be provided to those "of the best, most promising genius."[35] Scholarship students would be narrowed so that in Jefferson's elitist description "twenty of the best geniuses will be raked from the rubbish annually."[36] One would then be selected to attend the College of William & Mary. Jefferson's plan was rejected by the Virginia General Assembly, but it kept the notion of public schooling alive.

Jefferson was well schooled. He attended early schools taught by ministers and received his college education from the College of William & Mary. One biographer described his college years as a time when he excelled as a "promising classical scholar."[37] One indication of his voracious intellectual appetite was his huge library (some 6,700 books), which he sold to Congress and which then became the nucleus of the Library of Congress.[38]

Jefferson was an authentic man of letters. His book, *Notes on the State of Virginia,* has been hailed as a masterpiece of American literature.[39] On the surface the book is a treatise on his native state and combines history, government and environment, but Jefferson's highly literate and insightful style transforms the tome into a literary classic. Moreover, Jefferson's competence as an architect gained him wide acclaim to this day. A 1976 poll of American architects ranked Jefferson's designs for the University of Virginia and his home, Monticello, above those of such architectural giants as Frank Lloyd Wright and Louis Sullivan.[40]

As president his emphasis on education was minimal. He signed bills to appropriate lands for colleges in the western states and to establish West Point military academy. In his last message to Congress in 1808, he suggested that monies from a budget surplus could be used for education and other improvements such as canals and roads that would create the "great foundations of prosperity and union."[41]

In 1806, Jefferson called for a constitutional amendment to establish a federal role in education (see chapter 7). Nevertheless, his biographers failed to mention Jefferson's pursuit of the project. Indeed, Jefferson's interest in a national university reflected the ambivalent role he was to play as president on educational matters. Since Jefferson failed to believe that education had constitutional sanction, his efforts on behalf of a national university were half-hearted at best. He encouraged Joel Barlow to draft a prospectus for a national university for Congress' consideration. However, when Senator George Logan introduced a bill based on the Barlow prospectus, Jefferson did not press for enactment.[42]

What was Jefferson's impact on American education? The evidence appears mixed. Jefferson's educational plan for Virginia influenced state education systems. The University of Virginia was a model for state universities until the Morrill Land Grant Act of 1862 and the creation of state agricultural colleges. Jefferson's influence in the Northwest Ordinance of 1784 set policy guidelines for the federal government's involvement in education by giving surplus lands; this concept lasted well into the nineteenth century. Indeed, educational historian Lawrence Cremin credits "the influence of Jefferson's educational thought, during the nineteenth and into the twentieth" centuries as being "powerful and pervasive."[43]

Other historians conclude that "Jefferson's influence on American education was limited."[44] Historian Joseph F. Kett, from Jefferson's own University of Virginia, is more critical of Jefferson's impact on education. For Kett, Jefferson "may have had the right ideas, but they were in the wrong place and at the wrong time."[45] Kett cites the decline of the University of Virginia as a model of a university. The University of Virginia, after the Civil War, was not even mentioned in 1869 by influential Charles W. Eliot, president of Harvard, as a model for the "new education" at the university level.

However, Jefferson has persisted as the very model of an education president. (This image in 1988 partially persuaded President George Bush to hold the first Governors Conference on education at the University of Virginia.) Kett concludes that Jefferson's strong interest in education helped create a "legacy in the sense that an image of Jefferson has often inspired and propelled educational reformers."[46]

EDUCATION BEFORE THE CIVIL WAR

After Madison's unsuccessful attempt for a national university, presidential interest in education waned until Lincoln and the Morrill Land Grant Act of 1862. Madison's successor, James Monroe (1817-1825), favored a national university as did his successor, John Quincy Adams, but feared the constitutional issue.

Nevertheless, this period of American educational history was fertile. Symbolized by educator Horace Mann of Massachusetts, the aim was for universal public schooling, and the underlying rationale was still to educate citizens for democracy. "Never will wisdom preside in the halls of legislation," Mann declared "until common schools . . . create a far-seeing intelligence and a purer morality than has ever yet existed among the communities of men."[47]

The age of Jackson spurred educational reform. Andrew Jackson's (1829-1837) election to the presidency brought a revolution toward greater democracy. This occurred at a time of great national prosperity as America's economic independence in agriculture and manufacturing resulted from the War of 1812.

The Jackson influence on education was mainly symbolic of this greater emphasis on democracy. Jackson had little interest in education. His only references to education in his letters referred to the academic progress of his children, and none of his biographers credits him with major influence in education. His only passing reference to it was in his first annual message to Congress in 1829, when he advocated using a possible budget surplus for educational ends.

Jackson was a staunch advocate of states' rights. Consequently, in his message he hoped that a possible reduction of the national debt would result in a surplus that would have "the fiscal powers of the State increased, and maybe more extensively exerted in favor of education and other public objects."[48] For Jackson there would be no presidential role in education since he believed that the governing of "our internal affairs was intended to be left where the Federal Convention found it—in the state governments."[49] Still, his leadership for democratic reform nationwide had a rippling effect on the movement for common public schools, which educators such as Horace Mann sought.

ABRAHAM LINCOLN AND THE ECONOMY

With the advent of Abraham Lincoln and the Civil War, the ideological scenario shifted from education for democracy to education for the economy. The Morrill Land Grant bill of 1862, which Lincoln signed into law, had deep implications for the economy. At a time when the Industrial Revolution was taking place with a greater emphasis on manufacturing, there was concern over shoring up a sagging agricultural economy. The Land Grant Act provided for a system of state agricultural colleges that would directly impact on America's agriculture. It was the first major national link between education and the American economy.

Moreover, the act was another periodic presidential involvement in education. Lincoln's interest in education was minimal. Indeed, as a state representative to the Illinois legislature, he had opposed educational legislation, and as president, his only other connection with education dealt with the education of blacks in the newly freed territories during the Civil War. In that regard, his generals were more influential than he was. Still, his signing of the Morrill Land Grant Act was a major turning point in American educational history.

Lincoln reflected the nineteenth-century educational attitudes of the archetypical, self-educated man who explored the West. Rising from poverty, he did not attend formal schooling for more than a whole year in the aggregate. Elected to the Illinois House of Representatives in 1834, he began reading for the law. Lincoln was representative of many of the self-educated and self-reliant men of the American frontier.

It was natural, therefore, that he praised the virtues of self-education rather than those of the schoolhouse. He believed that all one had to do was read on one's own to obtain a decent education. On the learning of the law, for example, Lincoln counseled that one need "only to get the books, and read, and study carefully."[50]

Nevertheless, in his first political campaign he extolled formal schooling. He considered that education was "the most important subject" and that he "would be gratified to have in my power to contribute something to the advancement" of education.[51] However, Lincoln's reasons for the promotion of education had more to do with a citizenry informed on America's political institutions than with education's having any economic, political or social value. He hoped that education would enable Americans "to read the histories" so that they "may duly appreciate the value of our free institutions."[52]

This oft-quoted campaign speech gave the impression to many biographers of Lincoln that he was a champion of education. But, according to one scholar, for the most part Lincoln "showed indifference if not outright opposition toward the public support of education" in his deeds in office.[53] Eugene F. Provenzo, Jr., has convincingly argued that Lincoln in the Illinois state house and later in the U.S. Congress and as president at times actually opposed educational interests.

In his tenure from 1834 to 1842 in the Illinois legislature, Lincoln consistently opposed education bills.[54] After his election to Congress in 1846, Lincoln's involvement ceased until he became president of the United States.

As President, Lincoln made scant mention of education. His only references dealt with the education of blacks.[55] Most importantly, he was not directly involved in the passage of the Morrill Land Grant Act. He signed the Morrill bill into law without comment, and he did not mention the act in his next State of the Union message.[56] Edward Danforth Eddy, Jr., the historian of the Morrill Act, characterized Lincoln as a "man undoubtedly ahead of his times"; however, "new education in agriculture . . . had never been one of his strong concerns."[57]

Still, Lincoln played a key role in signing the bill. Indeed, his predecessor, James Buchanan, had vetoed the proposal in 1859 in deference to Southern and Western congressmen. When the bill was resubmitted in 1862, Lincoln was free of Southern pressure because of secession and the Civil War. Nevertheless, Eddy concluded that Lincoln signed the measure because "it was part of the progressive legislation pattern and philosophy to which he gave leadership."[58]

Although the land grant movement was educating only 20,000 students by the end of the century, the Morrill Land Grant Act had revolutionary implications for American higher education.[59] First, it enabled the states to establish state universities that would concentrate on agriculture and the mechanical arts and that would thus have a strong relationship to the development of the economy. Federal public lands were given to the states to create sixty-nine such state institutions of higher learning. In a nation that was rapidly transforming itself into a manufacturing nation during the sweep of the Industrial Revolution, the Morrill Act sought to aid the agricultural sector. State land grant institutions would play a key role in applying the advance of science to agricultural development.

Second, the Morrill Act was egalitarian in thrust. It opened the university doors, with open admission policies, to students of less privileged backgrounds. Third, the land grant colleges were a philosophical departure from the strictly academic groves. The development of the American service university would take the fruits of the ivory tower into the agricultural marketplace.

Fourth, the Morrill Act was a radical departure from previous federal intervention. It was a response to a national economic need; moreover, the act differed in its specificity from previous federal involvement.

In sum, the Morrill Land Grant Act was a national response to a national educational and economic issue. Despite his traditional indifference to education that stemmed from this background, Lincoln played an important role in signing the bill.

LINCOLN AND THE EDUCATION OF BLACKS

Lincoln's only other involvement as president involved the education of freed slaves. In this respect, his role left much to be desired.

Lincoln's Emancipation Proclamation of January 1, 1863, gave slaves freedom and accelerated the number of slaves escaping to the North, flooding refugee camps and causing a crisis of resettlement. Lincoln's generals perceived the need for the education of these former slaves. The South had denied 4 million blacks the opportunity to read and write, fearing that knowledge would breed discontent.[60] Many Union generals made appeals to citizens in the North to help teach these former slaves. The most influential appeal was made by General W.T. Sherman. In February 1862 he called upon the conscience of the North to "enable blacks to support and govern themselves" through a "suitable system of cultivation and instruction."[61]

Numerous benevolent societies in Northern cities responded to these appeals and sent teachers as well as food and money to the areas newly freed by the Union armies. Thus the freedmen's schools were born. By 1869 there were nearly 10,000 of these teachers in every part of the South.[62] The teachers sought to create a "complete school system for freedmen."[63] The former slaves in these schools were the first generation of blacks to read and write.

In 1865, one month before the war's conclusion, Congress created a freedman's bureau to institutionalize these efforts. Thus, according to a historian of black education, "Northern teachers of Negroes had gained the protection of union guns."[64]

Lincoln's role was ambivalent and to a certain extent detrimental to these efforts. His lenient amnesty policy permitted many Southern states to undermine the efforts of the freedman's schools. On December 8, 1863, Lincoln issued his Proclamation of Amnesty and Reconstruction. He permitted the rebellious states to determine much of their own course in Reconstruction. With respect to the education of blacks, Lincoln feebly suggested to the states that it was a course that he would not object to, but he gave the states final power. In this section of the amnesty proclamation he stated:

And I do further proclaim, and make known that any provision which may be adopted by such State government in relation to the freed people of such State, which shall recognize and declare their permanent freedom, *provide for their education*, and which may yet be consistent, as a temporary arrangement, with their present condition as a laboring landless, and homeless class, *will not be objected to* by the national executive (emphasis added).[65]

This backhanded endorsement of a policy to educate blacks was sufficient for the Southern states to derail temporarily the efforts of the freedmen's schools. "Black Codes" were adopted in many Southern states to replace the "Slave Codes." However, Congress reacted sharply to the Lincoln-Johnson leniency in Reconstruction by reinstituting national control to a large degree.

EDUCATION AND THE GILDED AGE

Despite the economic prosperity brought by the Industrial Revolution after the Civil War, American presidents did not realize, for the most part, the importance of education to the economy. Indeed, President James Garfield, for example, saw little value in the agricultural state colleges created by the Morrill Land Grant Act. It was not until the emergence of World War I that Wilson perceived the importance of an educated work force for America's economy.

One main reason for the lack of correlating education and the economy in the minds of our chief executives was the nature of this nascent industrial capitalism. The major industries that developed were ones, like iron, steel and the railroads, that prized brawn over brains. There were some technological breakthroughs such as the telegraph, telephone and electric light; however, economic development sought unskilled labor more than those highly educated. At the turn of the century slightly over 2 percent of college-age youth were in institutions of higher education.

Some presidents flirted with education. We shall look at their involvement.

JAMES A. GARFIELD (1881)

In contrast to Lincoln, James A. Garfield was a product of the frontier who believed in schooling. He enjoyed a distinguished career as an educator before entering politics. Most importantly, he was largely responsible as congressman for the creation of the U.S. Office of Education, which in 1979 became the Department of Education. However, he was in office barely a year when an assassin's bullet ended his life. Consequently, as president Garfield had little impact on education.

Garfield was born on the Ohio frontier, where his parents were farmers, and was the youngest of four children. His father died when he was two and left his mother to cope with frontier poverty. She decided that James' bright intellect deserved further education and hoped, according to one biographer, "that he might reach the high-place of a teacher or even a preacher."[66]

Garfield attended the local academy and later Williams College in Massachusetts. He uttered the famous quote about Williams College president Mark Hopkins, a nationally known educator: "Give me a log hut, with only a simple bench, Mark Hopkins on one end and I on the other, and you may have all the buildings, apparatus and libraries without him."[67]

Williams College was a high point in Garfield's life, and he returned to Ohio to become a teacher at the forerunner of Hiram College. In a short time, he was appointed president of this college. His interest in education was thus deep; however, he saw no especial economic value in education. "I do not believe in a college to educate men for the profession of farming," he wrote.[68]

His main credential in education was that he helped establish the U.S. Office of Education. In 1866, Garfield introduced a bill to create this agency with the express purpose to collect data on education throughout the states. He was influential not only in the passage of the bill but in his persuasive argument to retain it after controversy arose over a report issued by its first commissioner, Henry Barnard. Barnard's study condemned the mediocre education in many states and caused a political furor in the House that Garfield was able to calm.[69] Had he lived, Garfield as president may have had more of a national impact on education.

WOODROW WILSON (1913–1921)

With the advent of World War I and the need for industrial production, President Woodrow Wilson had some concern for the role of education in the American economy. It was decidedly a minor concern, however, and one is hard put to find any reference to Wilson's views on the matter in the biographies of him.

Wilson was first and foremost a scholar; moreover, he was the product of a scholarly family. Both his father and uncle were combination minister-scholars. Wilson attended Princeton as an undergraduate and obtained a law degree from the University of Virginia and a doctorate in history from Johns Hopkins. He was an average student at Princeton and Virginia but distinguished himself with his doctoral dissertation at Johns Hopkins, later published as *Congressional Government*.[70] Wilson followed this achievement with eight more works, including a biography of George Washington and a multivolume history of the United States.

He initially became a professor of history at elite Eastern colleges and rose to the presidency of Princeton University. As president of Princeton, he was a conservative reformer who sought to upgrade its intellectual life. He founded the Graduate College at Princeton and was embroiled in a controversial attempt to restructure club life to permit a more scholarly atmosphere. Wilson's views on Princeton's clubs were harsh and angered many on the Board of Trustees. He claimed: "The side shows are so numerous, so diverting—so important if you will—that they have swallowed up the circus."[71]

For Wilson, the college was "meant for a severe, more definite discipline ...[for] some intelligent and effective use of the mind."[72] He failed to persuade the Board of Trustees and, eventually, was forced to leave Princeton. However, despite his many academic accomplishments, Wilson had a lifelong love of politics and successfully ran for governor of New Jersey and later president of the United States.

The important educational legislation passed during Wilson's tenure as president dealt with vocational education. Although he played a small role in the legislation, he did recognize its economic value to the coming American war effort. The two bills that he urged Congress to pass and that he signed were the Smith-Lever Act of 1914, extending agricultural education, and the Smith-Hughes Act of 1917 establishing vocational education. Wilson termed the Smith-Lever Act, "one of the most significant and far-reaching measures for the education of adults ever adopted by a government."[73]

The Smith-Hughes Act of 1917 had strong industrial implications. Introduced in 1914, the bill met the usual controversy over federal control over education, but the imminence of war helped pass it through Congress. The bill established, for the first time, vocational education as a federal concern by promoting vocational education, financing the preparation of vocational teachers and establishing a federal Vocational Board of Education.

Wilson understood the economic importance of the Smith-Hughes Act. In his first annual message to Congress in 1916, he urged the House of Representatives to follow the lead of the Senate in approving the bill, which he thought was "of vital importance to the whole country because it concerns a matter, too long neglected upon which the thorough industrial preparation of the country for the critical years of economic development immediately ahead of us in very large measure depends."[74]

Despite his recognition of the economic importance of education in some areas, Wilson clung to the nineteenth-century belief of education for democracy. In 1918 at the height of World War I, Wilson reiterated this theme to the nation's teachers. He reminded them that "instruction in patriotism has always been a duty in American schools."[75] He pleaded with them to "acquire a deep spiritual understanding of the fundamental principles of our Government" since "the country must rely chiefly on you to interpret America to the children of the new generations."[76] For Wilson, America was the keeper of the democratic flame. Thus he told the nation's teachers:

Under your instruction the children should be made to understand the stern duty and the supreme privilege which belong to the United States of being chief interpreter to the world of those democratic principles which we believe to constitute the only force which can rid the world of injustice and bring peace and happiness to mankind.[77]

Wilson's energies were mostly devoted to World War I and the attempt to secure world peace through the creation of a League of Nations.

HERBERT HOOVER (1929–1933)

Herbert Hoover was another president who flirted with education. He sought to have the Office of Education elevated to cabinet status, a project that educators were able to achieve only some fifty years later.

Hoover's background combined education with science. He was orphaned by the time he was eleven. His father, a successful farm equipment merchant, died when Herbert was six; his mother died four years later. However, Hoover's mother had sufficiently provided for the education of her children by leaving a sizable sum sufficient to pay for college.[78]

As a result, Hoover attended Stanford University, where he became an engineer specializing in geology. As a successful mining engineer he helped found Stanford's School of Business to show his appreciation to his alma mater. He published a standard text on mining and later wrote books on political topics.

As president, Hoover sought to elevate the Office of Education into department status. One of his first acts was to appoint a National Advisory Commission on Education, comprised of fifty educators, to consider national educational policy. In his first annual message to Congress in 1929, Hoover stated that "in view of the considerable difference of opinion as to the policies which should be pursued by the Federal government, I have appointed a committee which is representative of the important educational associations . . . to investigate and present recommendations."[79]

Hoover added that a reorganization of educational services was necessary. In the same annual message, he informed Congress that cabinet reorganization was a "subject [which] . . . has been under consideration over 20 years."[80] He pointed out that "the conservation of national resources is spread among eight agencies in five departments . . . [and] the same may be said of educational services."[81]

Hoover's National Advisory Committee on Education issued a report that proved controversial. It called for more national control but stopped short of prescribing a national curriculum. Moreover, the committee recommended a separate Department of Education, which Hoover favored. Congress ignored both the committee's and the president's recommendations.[82] Hoover's interest in education was superseded by the complex problems presented by the most serious economic collapse in America's history.

CONCLUSION

Presidential interest in education until World War II was periodic. The first—and most intense—interest took place at the creation of the republic. The emphasis was on national involvement to support the theme of educating citizens to the new democracy. There was no economic consideration in the pleas of our founding fathers for an educational system.

The major exception in the nineteenth century was the passage of the Morrill Land Grant Act, which girded an agricultural system challenged by the rise of industry. As that Industrial Revolution progressed to the beginning of the twentieth century, few presidents were aware of a need for education in the new order. However, that realization escalated with the advent of World War II.

NOTES

1. Benjamin Rush to Nathaniel L. Greene, April 15, 1782, in *Letters of Benjamin Rush,* vol. 1, ed. L.H. Butler Field (Princeton, N.J.: Princeton University Press, 1951), p. 269.

2. Ibid., p. 413.

3. Ibid.

4. Thomas Jefferson, "A Bill for the More General Diffusion of Knowledge," in *Basic Writings of Thomas Jefferson,* ed. Philip S. Foner (Garden City, N.Y.: Halcyon House, 1944), p. 40.

5. George Washington, "Farewell Address," in *Basic Writings of George Washington,* ed. Saxe Commins (New York: Random House, 1948), p. 637.

6. Ibid.

7. James Madison to W.T., August 4, 1822, in *The Writings of James Madison,* vol. 9, ed. Gaillard Hunt (New York: Doubleday, 1910), pp. 107-8.

8. Lawrence A. Cremin, *American Education: The National Experience, 1783-1876* (New York: Harper and Row, 1980), p. 122.

9. Samuel Knox, "An Essay on the Best System of Liberal Education, Adapted to the Genius of the Government of the United States (1789), in *Essays on Education in the Early Republic,* ed. Frederick Rudolph (Cambridge, Mass.: Harvard University Press, 1965), p. 308.

10. Ibid., p. 318.

11. Ibid., p. 319.

12. Ibid., p. 312.

13. Samuel Harrison Smith, "Remarks on Education," in Rudolph, *Essays on Education in the Early Republic,* p. 210.

14. Ibid.

15. Ibid., p. 212.

16. Ibid., p. 213.

17. James Madison, *Journal of the Federal Convention* (Freeport, N.Y.: Books for Libraries Press, 1970), p. 726.

18. Field, *Letters of Benjamin Rush,* p. 491.

19. Ibid., p. 494.

20. George Washington, "Message to Congress on a National University, January 8, 1790" in *American Higher Education: A Documentary History,* vol. 1, ed. Richard Hofstader and Wilson Smith (Chicago: University of Chicago Press, 1961), pp. 157-58.

21. James Madison, "Message to Congress on a National University, 1810," in Hofstader and Smith, *American Higher Education: A Documentary History,* pp. 176-77.

22. Ibid., p. 177.

23. *Annals of Congress,* 14th Congress, 2d session (Washington, D.C.: U.S. Government Printing Office, 1817).

24. Ibid.

25. Ibid.

26. Ibid., p. 260.

27. Ibid., p. 268.

28. Ibid., p. 1063.

29. Ibid., p. 1064.

30. Ibid.

31. Ibid.

32. Alf J. Mapp, Jr., *Thomas Jefferson: A Strange Case of Mistaken Identity* (New York: Madison Books, 1987), p. 159.

33. John C. Henderson, *Thomas Jefferson: Views on Education* (New York: AMS Press, 1970), p. 39.

34. Mapp, *Thomas Jefferson,* p. 125.

35. Ibid.

36. Ibid.

37. Ibid., p. 15.

38. Henderson, *Thomas Jefferson: Views on Education,* p. 337.

39. Mapp, *Thomas Jefferson,* p. 160.

40. Ibid., p. 162.

41. Thomas Jefferson, *The Writings of Thomas Jefferson,* vol. 8 (Washington, D.C.: Taylor and Maury, 1856), p. 110.

42. Joseph F. Kett, "Thomas Jefferson and Education," in *Thomas Jefferson: A Reference Biography,* ed. Merrill D. Peterson (New York: Charles Scribner's Sons, 1986), p. 240.

43. Cremin, *American Education: The National Experience,* p. 114.

44. Kett, "Thomas Jefferson and Education," p. 250.

45. Ibid.

46. Ibid.

47. As quoted in Cremin, *American Education: The National Experience,* p. 137.

48. Francis Newton Thorpe, ed., *The Statesmanship of Andrew Jackson: As Told in His Writings and Speeches* (New York: Tandy and Thomas, 1909), p. 50.

49. Ibid., p. 51.

50. Eugene F. Provenzo, Jr., "Lincoln and Education," *Educational Studies,* Summer 1982, p. 198.

51. Ibid., p. 193.

52. Ibid.

53. Ibid., p. 199.

54. Ibid., p. 196.

55. Ibid., p. 198.

56. Ibid., p. 199.

57. Edward Danforth Eddy, Jr., *Colleges for Our Land and Time: The Land-Grant Idea in American Education* (New York: Harper and Brothers, 1957), p. 35.

58. Ibid.

59. Ibid., p. 116.

60. Ruskin Teeter, *The Opening Up of American Education* (New York: University Press of America, 1983), p. 69.

61. As quoted in Henry Allen Bullock, *A History of Negro Education in the South: From 1616 to the Present* (Cambridge, Mass.: Harvard University Press, 1967), p. 19.

62. Ruskin Teeter, *The Opening Up of American Education,* p. 67.

63. Henry Allen Bullock, *A History of Negro Education in the South: From 1616 to the Present* (Cambridge, Mass.: Harvard University Press, 1967), p. 23.

64. Ibid.

65. Abraham Lincoln, "Proclamation of Amnesty and Reconstruction; December 8, 1863," in *The Collected Works of Abraham Lincoln, Volume VII, 1863-1864* ed. Roy P. Basker (New Brunswick, N.J.: Rutgers University Press, 1953), p. 55.

66. Robert Granville Caldwell, *James A. Garfield: Party Chieftain* (Hamden, Conn.: Archon Books, 1965), p. 13.

67. As quoted in Caldwell, *James A. Garfield,* p. 185.

68. Ibid.

69. Ibid., p. 186.

70. Henry Wilkinson Bragdon, *Woodrow Wilson: The Academic Years* (Cambridge, Mass.: Harvard University Press, 1967).

71. Woodrow Wilson, "What Is a College for?" *Scribner's Magazine* 46, no. 5 (November 1909), pp. 576-77.

72. Ibid., p. 577.

73. As quoted in Americo D. Lapti, *Education and the Federal Government* (New York: Mason/Charter, 1975), p. 97.

74. Arthur S. Link, ed., *The Papers of Woodrow Wilson,* vol. 40 (Princeton, N.J.: Princeton University Press, 1982), p. 159.

75. Ibid., p. 456.

76. Ibid., p. 455.

77. Ibid.

78. David Burner, *Herbert Hoover: A Public Life* (New York: Knopf, 1979), p. 11.

79. Herbert Hoover, "First Annual Message to Congress, December 3, 1929," in *The State Papers and Other Writings of Herbert Hoover,* vol. 1, ed. William Starr Meyers (Garden City, N.Y.: Doubleday and Doran, 1934), pp. 158-59.

80. Ibid., p. 162.

81. Ibid., p. 164.

82. Burner, *Herbert Hoover,* pp. 223-24.

3

Education for the Economy

By the end of World War II, American education had become a national concern. The emergence of an economy that was technological in nature brought with it an awareness of the need for an educated work force. The rise of America as a power in world affairs further correlated with a need to respond to educational needs. Consequently, American presidents increasingly began to view education in national terms.

In this chapter we shall examine the varying responses of these presidents to national issues in education. Since two of the presidents, Lyndon Johnson and Ronald Reagan, were in the forefront of large-scale educational reform movements, we shall consider their leadership and the reform movements in separate succeeding chapters.

THE ECONOMY: 1945–1975

The post–World War II age had long spells of economic prosperity. The forties, fifties and sixties had major periods of affluence. Unemployment was low, productivity was high and America enjoyed the role of a favorable trade balance in which exports exceeded imports. Concomitantly, America's national leaders could afford to invest in education. By the time massive poverty was rediscovered in the 1960s, the affluent two-thirds of Americans felt more compassionate toward the poor. As productivity declined in the seventies, the American economy began a slow decline.

For nearly three decades after World War II, America prospered. Perhaps the most popular economic analysis of the time was John Kenneth Galbraith's book aptly titled *The Affluent Society*. Published in 1958 as the American economy prospered, Galbraith's tome was a paean to America's

economic shrewdness and hard work. "Western man," Galbriath trium-
phantly announced, "has escaped for the moment the poverty which was
for so long his all-embracing fate."[1] Indeed, Galbraith noted that in the
United States the lowest fifth in the economic stratum enjoyed a 42 percent
rise in income in the short decade between 1941 and 1950.[2]

For Galbraith, productivity was the key. "It is the increase in output in
recent decades," he wrote, "which has brought the great material increase,
the well-being of the average man."[3] Consequently, the age of affluence saw
that "insecurity was eliminated in the real world."[4]

Most importantly, during this economic boom the American economy
changed. After World War II, America became primarily a service economy
rather than a goods-producing economy. Sociologist Daniel Bell noted in
his study, *The Coming of the Post-Industrial Society,* that at the turn of the
century only three in ten workers were in service industries.[5] He defined
goods-producing industries as agriculture, manufacturing and construction
and service industries as finance, transportation, profit service and government. In 1947, employment was evenly balanced between the goods-
producing and service industries. In 1968, six in ten workers were in service
industries.[6] Moreover, by 1956 the number of white-collar workers had
surpassed blue-collar workers.[7]

The implications for education were clear. The rise of sophisticated tech-
nologies changing the labor force meant a concomitant rise in education.
"The most striking aspect of the new labor force," Bell wrote, "is the level
of formal educational attainment."[8] After World War II, the G.I. Bill of
Rights ushered in mass higher education; nearly half of all cohort college-
age students at that time would eventually attend an institution of higher
learning. It was a response to an overwhelming need. "The major problem
for the post-industrial society," Bell forecast, "will be adequate numbers of
trained persons of professional and technical caliber."[9]

By the 1970s, the economy began a downward slide. According to economist Lester Thurow in *The Zero-Sum Society,* America began having a
"productivity problem."[10] A combination of forces contributed to a steady
decline in America's gross national product (GNP). High prices of imported
energy resulting from the Arab oil embargo of 1973 concomitantly led to
high prices for American goods. According to Thurow, a reluctance by
American business to invest in plant and equipment to modernize and to
introduce new products contributed to slow growth. Thurow characterized
the American economy as one "where the losses exactly equal the win-
nings."[11]

America's slow economic growth was challenged by the rapid growth of
Japan and West Germany. Between 1972 and 1978 industrial growth in
the United States rose only 1 percent per year whereas in Japan that growth
was over 5 percent per year.[12] America dropped from second to fifth place
in the world in the per capita GNP during that time. "Where the U.S.

economy had once generated the world's highest standard of living," Thurow concluded, "it was now well down the list and slipping farther each year."[13]

The result was stagflation at home. Stagflation was that odd combination of high inflation and high unemployment. Normally one reduces the other. In this 1970s economy, a high point of 9 percent unemployment was reached as the GNP fell.[14]

The national concern with educating the American work force eroded as the economy faltered. Popular educational books carried such titles as *The Case against College* (Caroline Bird) and *The Overeducated American* (Richard B. Freeman). As the economy stagnated, so did national interest in education reform.

EDUCATION AFTER WORLD WAR II

After World War II, America's leading educators sensed the metamorphosis in America's educational position. They demanded more national influence, first in the form of federal aid to education.[15] Political figures joined the chorus for increased national attention to education. This drumbeat continued in varying measure to the present day. Whereas the 1945 cry was for federal aid, the concern in 1990 was for national goals in education.

A pattern developed whereby domestic and international issues propelled American education to presidential attention. Major and minor national crises required educational responses. After World War II, the concern was over manpower resources. By the 1950s, a cold war with Soviet communism required a need to re-examine both American values in the ideological conflict and American scientific advances in the military.

The 1960s brought a concern for the poor, blacks and other minorities. The civil rights movement was the principal initiator of a major education reform movement focused on equality. This equality movement dominated national education policy for nearly two decades. By the 1980s, foreign economic competition ushered in an educational reform movement on excellence and on grooming a cadre of bright students to compete economically. In each case, educational issues had gone beyond the states into the national domain. Education had become a national concern, and the key player was the president of the United States.

The drive to nationalize American education was first fought on the issue of federal aid to education. First introduced into the Senate after World War II in 1946, nearly two dozen federal aid bills were unsuccessfully considered in Congress until the passage of the Elementary and Secondary Education Act of 1965.[16] Most of those bills were for school construction rather than for direct pupil needs.

Opposition to these bills emerged from three main sectors of American life. Southerners feared the dismantling of de jure segregated schools, the Catholic church opposed any federal aid that did not provide also for Catholic schools, and many politicians feared federal control of education.

Presidents varied in their support of federal aid. Liberals like Roosevelt and moderates like Eisenhower were opposed to federal control. Others such as Truman, Kennedy and Johnson were strongly committed to federal aid and a federal presence in education.

FRANKLIN DELANO ROOSEVELT (1933–1945) AND HARRY S TRUMAN (1945–1953) AND THE RIGHT TO EDUCATION

Franklin Delano Roosevelt's contribution to education as a national issue was substantive in its impact. First, Roosevelt was responsible for the G.I. Bill of Rights, which provided subsidized higher education for veterans and ushered in the era of mass higher education. Second, Roosevelt introduced a crucial philosophical concept that emerged from the G.I. Bill of Rights process: the right to education.

Roosevelt was not especially education-minded. He benefitted from an elite education and attended prestigious Groton and Harvard University. He was a good student at both schools but did not leave with a penchant for the values of education, unlike his fellow Harvard graduate, John F. Kennedy, who did perceive the value of public education.[17]

The idea of the right to education was proposed by Roosevelt in a 1942 report on the development of natural resources. Roosevelt called for the extension of the Constitution's Bill of Rights. He wanted to add to the "old freedoms" some "new freedoms."[18] Among these "new freedoms," Roosevelt enunciated the eighth of nine "new freedoms": "the right to education."[19] Roosevelt proposed "the right to education for work, for citizenship and for personal growth and happiness."[20]

The first of the "new freedoms" was the "the right to work," revealing the imprint the Great Depression still held in wartime America.[21] Other rights dealt with fair pay, "the right to adequate food, clothing, shelter and medical care," security, free enterprise, "the right to equality," rest and recreation.[22] It was the right to education, however, that dominated the policy debate after World War II. Educational historian Diane Ravitch observed that the right to college constituted the third "great struggle" of American education—the first having been the establishment of the public school and the second the emergence of high school as a universal experience.[23]

Roosevelt's idea of a right to education was pursued by his successor, Harry S Truman. In 1947, Truman created a Commission on Higher Education to study the issue of universal higher education. In a series of reports, the commission proclaimed education to be "the foundation of democratic liberties."[24] Most importantly, the "democratic creed...assumes [educa-tion] to be their [Americans'] birthright; an equal chance with all others to make the most of their native abilities."[25] The commission estimated that at least 49 percent of the American public possessed the native ability to complete fourteen years of schooling—including two years of college. The authors of the report believed that fully one-third of all Americans had the mental capacity to obtain a college degree. Consequently, the commission recommended educational policies that would enable students to achieve these goals without encountering an "insuperable economic barrier."[26]

The Truman commission report was well received by the American media. The *New York Times* concluded that the report "may well become a land-mark in the history of higher education."[27] *Life* magazine called the right to education "a civic birthright" and stated that "a basic principle of Amer-ican democracy is the more education the better."[28]

The concept of the right to education lingered. Lyndon Johnson com-missioned a study in the last days of his administration—the "508" study—estimating the federal cost of free education to the fourteenth year.[29] This study was followed by three studies in 1970, 1971 and 1973 by the Carnegie Commission on Equality in Higher Education that recommended free access to fourteen years of schooling.[30]

This concept of the right to education rested on shaky constitutional grounds. Indeed, thirty years after Roosevelt endorsed the idea, the United States Supreme Court ruled that education was not a right but a privilege under the Constitution. In a school finance case, Justice Lewis Powell de-livered the majority opinion that dealt a severe blow to those advocates of the right to education. He wrote that "education, of course, is not among the rights afforded explicit protection under our Federal constitution."[31] Moreover, Powell determined that there was not "any basis" for its being "implicitly so protected."[32]

Still, the idea persisted. In the 1988 Democratic presidential primary campaign, the Reverend Jesse Jackson made the right to college a key cam-paign issue. More importantly, presidents since Roosevelt have sub rosa adhered to a policy that endorsed the right-to-college idea. They have ad-vocated policies that would enable qualified students to have access to college regardless of ability to pay.

Two major economic developments affected educational policy during the Roosevelt-Truman years. First, there was the rise of the technological state. Sophisticated technology required an increasingly well-educated work force. For the Truman Commission on Higher Education, education was no less than the "biggest and most hopeful of the Nation's enterprises."[33] The authors spoke of the "critical need" of higher education "in the light of the social role" of higher education.[34] Indeed, the thesis of the commis-sion's report was that technology and industrialization required higher de-grees of educational preparedness.

The other economic variable was the specter of unemployment. The scars of the Great Depression of the 1930s were not completely healed. Despite the emergence of prosperity after World War II, Roosevelt's analysts had predicted a down economy after the war as returning veterans flooded the job market. Estimates ranged as high as 8 or 9 million unemployed.[35] Such mass unemployment did not take place. One reason was that an unpredicted number of veterans chose to attend college on Roosevelt's G.I. Bill of Rights.

Unemployment, however, was the main domestic issue on the minds of Roosevelt and Truman. Roosevelt pledged in November 1943 that "the first task after the war is to provide employment [to our veterans]... and our demobilized war workers."[36]

Truman echoed the theme. In his first State of the Union message in 1945, he predicted that "obviously... there will be a great deal of unemployment."[37] The chief task of the federal government, therefore, would be to "assist industry to reconvert to peacetime production as quickly and effectively as possible."[38] It was a theme he was to repeat in the next year's State of the Union message. He feared "serious consequences" in the event that America could not fulfill "the need for full production and full employment at home."[39]

By 1947, the economy had greatly improved. In his State of the Union message, Truman happily reported that "the state of our national economy presents great opportunities for all."[40] Most importantly, he declared that "we have virtually full employment."[41] Never again would the Great Depression loom large in America's mind.

THE G.I. BILL OF RIGHTS

The embodiment of the concept of the right to college was the G.I. Bill of Rights. Conceived during the Roosevelt administration, the bill enabled returning World War II veterans to attend college on government subsidies. It is interesting to note that the bill was one of "rights," reflecting the prevailing thinking by the president and leading educational advisers.

Roosevelt can be credited with a major role in developing the G.I. Bill of Rights. He created the National Resources Planning Board in 1939, which served as a policy arm. He was instrumental in drafting board policy with his nine "new rights," including education, and he publicly declared that he wanted education to be an important component of any program for returning veterans.[42]

The National Resources Planning Board appointed a smaller committee of educators and military personnel to consider benefits for returning service personnel. Roosevelt was convinced that education should be a vital part of the program. Although he sought to avoid publicity over the pending veterans' program, he made one exception in 1942 when he announced that a "committee of educators" was considering a program that would allow "young men whose education has been interrupted to resume their schooling and afford equal opportunity for the training and education for other young men of ability after their service in the armed forces comes to an end."[43]

Nevertheless, Roosevelt preferred not to lobby strenuously for the administration's version of the bill. Since the American Legion had a somewhat similar version, he preferred the veterans' organization to "keep the initiative" and successfully lobby for its bill in Congress.[44] Nonetheless, Roosevelt's developing broad policy and the initiation of his policy group in devising the first proposal are sufficient to credit him with a key role in the G.I. Bill of Rights.

The G.I. Bill of Rights transformed American higher education. Prior to the passage of the bill, college was a privilege, for the most part, of the affluent. There were minor exceptions, such as the free universities in New York City and California, but, as a rule, the poor were unable to attend college. The G.I. Bill changed that situation and enabled over 2 million World War II and Korean veterans to take advantage of higher education. Today, nearly 50 percent of high school students attend some form of higher education—the targeted figure of the Truman Commission on Higher Education.[45]

However, few predicted the impact of the G.I. Bill. Policy makers had envisioned only a small number of veterans taking advantage of the educational benefits. Ten years after the G.I. Bill was passed, 2,232,000 veterans had attended college under its provisions.[46] Mass education had arrived.

The G.I. Bill provoked little public response when passed in 1944. According to the historian of the bill, Keith Olson, no major newspaper in the nation carried an editorial on the G.I. Bill. Olson concluded that "the general public overlooked or underestimated the G.I. Bill."[47]

However, some in the academic community were alarmed. President James B. Conant of Harvard decried the "distressing" nature of the G.I. Bill.[48] He feared that colleges "may find the least capable among the war generation," who would be "flooding the facilities of higher education."[49] President Robert Maynard Hutchins of the University of Chicago seconded Conant's apprehensions about the G.I. Bill. Maynard wrote an article for the popular weekly *Collier's* entitled "The Threat to American Education."[50]

The "threat" turned into a pleasant surprise. The returning veterans possessed greater maturity and motivation than the average college student. Veterans earned higher grades and were less likely to fail than their counterparts.[51] Studies indicated that these veterans, despite some with poor academic preparation, were, in the words of the business magazine *Fortune*, "the best . . . the most mature . . . the most responsible . . . and the most self-disciplined group of students ever."[52]

The G.I. Bill encompassed more than education. The bill dealt with unemployment compensation, medical care and home and farm loans, but it is generally thought of as an education bill. Educationally the bill provided generous subsidies for the time. Each veteran who had served at least ninety days in the armed services was entitled to education equal to the time spent in uniform. The federal government paid tuition, fees and books to a maximum of $500. Moreover, living costs were subsidized so that married veterans received $75 a month and single veterans $50 a month.

Harry S Truman's contribution was in beginning the pressure for federal aid to education and continuing the concept of the right to education. Truman, having had so little of it himself, was not especially keen on education. His terminal degree was high school. He had hoped to attend West Point but was not nominated, and his family was not sufficiently well-off to afford a college education.[53] But, in post–World War II America, Truman could sense the growing importance of education to America's commonwealth.

Truman sponsored federal aid bills in 1947 and 1948. Poor relations with Congress, as well as the fact that America was not yet ready for federal intrusion into education, hampered his success. Some educators believed that Truman's proposals would primarily benefit private schools, and others mainly feared federal control.[54] In his memoirs, Truman recalled lambasting members of the Eightieth Republican Congress by asking them "to act upon vitally needed measures, such as aid to education, which they say they are for."[55] Scant mention of education is made in these memoirs primarily because the president's attempts were unsuccessful.

But the overriding factor in Truman's concern with education was the cold war, which was America's response to the growing influence of the Soviet Union and world communism. Under Truman, the United States sought to contain the rise of communism. This effort sometimes meant a "hot" war such as in Korea. The cold war entailed prolonged diplomatic, military and ideological hostility of the two great superpowers—the United States and the Soviet Union.

Truman perceived the need for an educated America to develop the technological skills to wage the cold war. "Education," he declared "is our first line of defense."[56] Specifically, he enlisted education in the cold war. "Through education alone," he said, "can we combat the tenets of communism."[57] For Truman, the "challenge of communist imperialism" required America to preserve its world leadership in science and industry, and "education and research are vital to the maintenance of this leadership."[58] Truman's successors—Dwight D. Eisenhower and John F. Kennedy—continued to mix the cold war with the educational needs of the nation.

Roosevelt had far-reaching impact with the G.I. Bill of Rights, which transformed American higher education, and Truman must be given credit for introducing and maintaining pressure for federal aid to education.

Other tumultuous events dominated their presidencies. For Roosevelt the Great Depression and World War II dominated. For Truman, there were the termination of the war, the beginning of cold war with communism and the Soviet Union and military conflict in Korea. Still, both presidents responded to a growing national awareness by educators and policy makers that education superseded state responsibility and must be addressed in a national context.

DWIGHT D. EISENHOWER (1953–1961) AND NATIONAL DEFENSE

Dwight D. Eisenhower was a president reluctant to involve himself in the national debate over education. He eschewed federal aid as a principle and showed little interest in education. However, the cold war propelled him into a strong role in education, first, with a response to the advanced state of the Soviet Union in space and second, in the continuing re-examination of American values taught by the schools in the face of the rising importance of world communism.

Eisenhower's main concern was the cold war. For him, his greatest presidential accomplishment, especially for a military man, was the ending of armed conflict in Korea and "waging peace."[59] Nevertheless, the launching of the first spacecraft by the Soviets in October 1957 thrust him squarely in the national education debate. He responded by advocating an "emergency role" of the federal government in education.[60] Global concerns had made education a national issue once again.

Eisenhower's qualifications for the presidency were his military record. He directed the Allies as supreme commander in the victory over Germany in Europe. His brief foray into education came after the war when he was made president of Columbia University, a post he had not sought; he had suggested his brother Milton, an educator, in his stead. But it proved instrumental as a political launching pad for him.

Consequently, Eisenhower was mostly a nonpresident at Columbia. He delegated most of the academic chores to subordinates and made rare public appearances to highlight some pet national issue. Much of his time he devoted to his military memoirs, *Crusade in Europe*. Many of Columbia's faculty held Eisenhower's intellectual capacities suspect.[61]

On October 4, 1957, during Eisenhower's second term, the Soviet Union was the first to launch a craft—Sputnik—into space. Sputnik set off hysteria in the minds of the American public. It was feared that the Russians, the arch cold war enemy, had gained superiority in the race in space and also, perhaps, in national defense. The immediate reaction of many political figures and educators was to blame the schools for America's inferior position in space.

Sputnik raised the question of whether the United States could lose the cold war. Until Sputnik, America believed in its economic, military and scientific superiority. Sputnik dramatically undermined that confidence.

The national response was not to blame the federal government for failing adequately to promote a space program; rather, the public schools were accused of failing to groom the "brainpower for the Cold War." The Sputnik debate was to echo in the 1980s with the excellence reform movement. Again, the failure of America to compete economically with foreign countries, especially Japan, was not laid at the door of poor management by American business; the public schools were the target for national reform.

The key was national security. America perceived Russian superiority in the space program as a vital threat to its survival, and President Eisenhower emphasized that threat repeatedly. Three months after Sputnik, the president gave a special message to Congress on the Sputnik crisis. He stressed that American education now faced "new responsibilities in the cause of freedom" because of the "national security interest in the quality and scope of our educational system."[62] Although reluctant, he injected the federal government into educational policy to play an "emergency role" in order to give "special . . . attention to education in science and engineering."[63]

Sputnik panicked America. Immediately after the Soviet launch, politicians and educators sounded the battle cry. Senator Henry Jackson (D-Wash.), a hard-line anticommunist, called Sputnik a "devastating blow to the United States."[64] The New York City Board of Education president bemoaned the jolt to the "national ego" that left America "all shook up."[65] For him the battle line was the schools, where teachers constituted "our first line of defense" and where "victory will be forged in your classrooms."[66]

The Sputnik fever spread. One month after the launch, a record 6,000 New York City higher school seniors flooded to college presentations on science and engineering.[67] One educator who wrote to the *New York Times* attempted to deflate the "hysteria of fear" that may lead to a "hope for miracles."[68]

As in the Japan worship that engulfed federal education officials in the 1980s, Russian schools were proclaimed far superior to those of the United States. A U.S. Office of Education two-year study on Soviet education was released one month after the launching of Sputnik. It portrayed Russian schoolchildren as spending a longer school year at required core courses in the sciences without electives. Moreover, it portrayed Russian discipline as "severe" and Soviet teachers as held in "high esteem," with some receiving extra pay "for extra work."[69]

The *New York Times* gave a glimpse of Soviet education as rigorous and strenuous. An article decrying "no snap course for young Ivan" detailed the full schedule of "hard" subjects in a six-day school week and observed that "it is not much fun to be a schoolboy in the Soviet Union."[70] Editorialists from the *New York Times* concluded that "from the point of view of our national security, there may well be some things about science and mathematics curricula that we can learn from the Russians."[71]

By contrast American schoolchildren—and the American public—were perceived as soft. Former president Harry S Truman bemoaned that "the trouble with Americans is that they are fat and lazy and want too many cars and too many fancy gadgets."[72] Only a few demurred from the critique of American schooling in the wake of Sputnik. Secretary of Health, Education and Welfare Marian B. Folsom opposed any radical restructuring of American education while conceding Soviet gains in science.[73]

The cold war permeated every aspect of American life. The defense budgets rose from 29.7 percent of the national budget in 1947 to 68 percent of the national budget by 1951 and remained steady at that figure for the next decade.[74] Many Americans agreed with Harvard president James B. Conant that it was the task of the schools to prepare students for their roles in the cold war. Nothing was more important than stressing American values in the great ideological war between capitalism and communism.

One of the prime educational targets was progressive education. After Sputnik, the attacks on progressive education escalated. Senator John W. Bricker, for example, blamed the space deficit on America's "professional pedagogues" who were "responsible for stunting the growth of young Americans" by inculcating "progressive education."[75]

Progressive education was the educational system developed by the eminent philosopher-educator John Dewey. At its best, it placed the child at the center of education and offered rich experiences to enable the individual to cope with society's demands. At its worst, progressive education devolved into simply life adjustment, with a heavy emphasis on socialization.

Those who warmly received Dewey's ideas were the National Education Association and, most importantly, prestigious colleges of education. In 1919, the Progressive Education Association was formed.[76] By the late 1940s, progressive education had been corrupted into life adjustment, and even Dewey repudiated what passed for his ideas, but it was an educational philosophy that did not seem suited for a cold war mentality.

Perhaps the most famous—and harshest—critic of progressive education was Admiral Hyman Rickover. Rickover was a nuclear physicist and engineer instrumental in our national defense. (He was also to be the chief mentor of future president Jimmy Carter.) Rickover seized upon the Sputnik hysteria to advance his ideas on education, which stressed the hard sciences.

Shortly after Sputnik, a collection of Rickover's speeches on American education was published under the provocative title *Education and Freedom*. Rickover proclaimed the schools as "our first line of defense."[77] Those schools, he charged, had let down America. The chief culprit was "progressive education," which had emphasized "life-adjustment teaching," which was "not as nearly as difficult as teaching algebra, French, or physics."[78]

With the advent of Sputnik, Rickover pointed out that America was "now faced with universal education of high caliber in Russia."[79] Consequently, Rickover declared that American educators could no longer "fool the American people into believing that education can safely be left to the 'professional' educators."[80]

Sputnik not only challenged progressive education but struck deep at cherished American values. Vice-President Richard Nixon, for example, complained that Americans should not react to Sputnik by attempting to become a "pale carbon copy of the scientific materialism" of communism.[81] Sputnik prompted an agonizing reappraisal of American values.

Two national reports highlighted that reappraisal. One was commissioned by President Eisenhower, and the other was commissioned by the Rockefeller Brothers Fund. Both struck similar themes of re-emphasizing traditional American values of individualism.

Confronted by a communist society that stressed a collective identity, America responded with its time-honored emphasis on the individual. The President's Commission on National Goals cited "the status of the individual," which "must remain our primary concern."[82] The Rockefeller Panel Reports, entitled *Prospects for America,* declared that "paradoxical though it may seem, society as a whole must come to the aid of the individual."[83]

Sputnik hovered in the background of the reports. *Prospects for America* worried that "for the first time in history, our survival is imperiled by the threat of technological inferiority."[84]

The educational sections of the two reports were written by John Gardner, president of the Carnegie Corporation. His recommendations reflected the influence of the Truman Commission on Higher Education. The goals of the president's reports were for two-thirds of America's youngsters to complete high school and one-third to graduate from college—figures achieved today. Moreover, Gardner called for increased spending on education on the federal, state and local levels.[85]

Eisenhower was swept up in the Sputnik hysteria. He wrote in his memoirs that "the Soviet scientific achievement was impressive."[86] In the first press conference after the Soviet launch, Eisenhower envisioned his role as "first the awakening of the United States" to the need "of increasing our scientific output of our colleges and universities."[87] The focus was on the performance of the schools rather than on the government's space program.

Federal interference created an ideological problem for Eisenhower. Opposed to a strong federal role, he still saw the need for some federal action. Still, the demand of America's educators was for general federal aid to education. Eisenhower summed up his position in his memoirs that he "was convinced that my objections to the concept of generalized and direct help for all higher education were sound."[88] In this regard, he was advised by such influential educators as Harvard president James B. Conant and Carnegie Foundation president John Gardner. Indeed, Eisenhower viewed the National Defense Education Act—his response to Sputnik—as part of a "trend toward federal dependency."[89]

Eisenhower did support three federal aid bills that would have provided construction loans.[90] But he believed any form of federal aid to education should be temporary and mainly a prod to state funding.[91] The Eisenhower philosophy of government rested on the cornerstones of less federal influence, sound fiscal policies with a balanced budget and the "waging of peace."

The National Defense Education Act (NDEA) of 1958 was President Eisenhower's and the Democratic Congress' reply to Sputnik. The heart of the act provided loan monies for students interested in science; however, the act clearly limited the federal role. The act stated that "an educational emergency exists and requires action by the federal government."[92] However, the act boldly added that "federal control of education [was] prohibited."[93] NDEA allocated $47.5 million each year from 1958 to a maximum of $90 million by 1962 for student loans. Undergraduates could borrow $1,000 per year to a $5,000 maximum over the course of their studies. National Defense Fellowships would go to graduate students, with a preference for college teachers. In the first year, 1,000 fellows would be selected, each to receive $1,500 in each succeeding year to 1962. For the first year, graduate students would receive $2,000 and $2,400 for each year to 1962. Other NDEA provisions included monies for language centers, institutes and college equipment in the assistance of the study of science, math and foreign languages.[94]

The National Defense Education Act of 1958 passed with relative ease. The Senate's handling of the matter was typical of post-Sputnik hysteria. Senator Lister Hill of Alabama, who introduced the Senate version, informed his colleagues of the gravity of the measure. NDEA, he said, "comes at a time of great decision. A severe blow—some would way a disastrous blow— has been struck at America's self-confidence and at her prestige in the world."[95]

Most importantly, Eisenhower's bill had significant bipartisan support. Senate majority leader Lyndon Johnson (D-Tex.) informed the Senate that he was "very much pleased and . . . very proud" of the Hill bill and hoped that "it will be debated and pass before we recess today."[96] Republican supporters included Javits of New York, who was "delighted with the bill."[97] Consequently, the Senate version passed by a vote of sixty-two to twenty-six.

There were opponents, but, for the most part, they objected mainly to a specific item in the bill. For example, Senator Strom Thurmond (D–S.C.) objected to the educational aid. This pattern was repeated in the House. The House-Senate Conference resulted in a compromise version of the two bills. The Senate passed the compromise by a vote of 66 to 15, and the House, 212 to 85.

Eisenhower's administrative style was that of the "hidden hand" presidency. He eschewed staff disputes and sought to remain above the battle and to set broad policy, as with NDEA. Moreover, a Mideast crisis over the Suez Canal and a developing scandal over his chief aide, Sherman Adams, preoccupied him during the passage of NDEA.[98]

NDEA had significant impact. By 1964, almost .75 million students had received NDEA monies. The historian of NDEA, Barbara Clowse, concluded that "enough men and women had taken advantage of the assistance to have influenced the United States educational system."[99]

Others were critical of Eisenhower's leadership during Sputnik. Eisenhower's biographer, Stephen Ambrose, although sympathetic to his subject, felt that Eisenhower's leadership in the Sputnik hysteria resulted in "a great opportunity wasted."[100] Ambrose argued that "Eisenhower could have used the post-Sputnik hysteria to vastly strengthen the educational system in the United States."[101]

Eisenhower was reluctantly thrust into a national role in education. His lack of interest in education and his political philosophy constricted his leadership role.

JOHN F. KENNEDY (1961–1963) AND FEDERAL AID

John F. Kennedy did not have any success in enacting a federal aid to education bill. The fact that the timing was not right to pass his legislative program, combined with his inability to persuade Congress, resulted in failure. Nevertheless, his constant pressure laid the groundwork for Lyndon Johnson's later success. Indeed, as one analyst observed, "What was refused during his lifetime was given freely after his death."[102]

John F. Kennedy had a strong interest in education. He attended elite private schools, understood the importance of education and possessed solid intellectual credentials. He published two historical books in his lifetime, which were well received. One book, *Profiles in Courage,* illustrating great acts of political independence in the U.S. Congress, won him the Pulitzer Prize in 1957. The book was widely read and established Kennedy as a man of intellect. One biographer claimed that this "recognition of intellectual and literary distinction meant more to Kennedy than any other honor."[103] The other book was a revision of his senior thesis at Harvard entitled *Why England Slept,* an analysis of Great Britain's military unpreparedness for World War II.

At Harvard, Kennedy's initial academic experience was lackluster, earning him a C average. His grades improved by his junior year as he majored in government, and his senior thesis received a magna cum laude so that he graduated from Harvard with honors in his major.

Kennedy carried this sophisticated intellectualism into the White House. For the first time, the White House was regularly opened to artists, scholars and intellectuals. His tenure was described as a revival of Camelot—the legendary court of King Arthur—and Kennedy was compared to Thomas Jefferson.

Federal aid to education was the cornerstone of Kennedy's New Frontier. Paul Light polled Kennedy aides on the major domestic concerns of the Kennedy administration. The highest number, 91 percent, cited federal aid to education as a major Kennedy priority.[104] This was followed by policy discussions of Medicare, unemployment and civil rights as the last policy issue, with only 18 percent mentioning civil rights.[105] Indeed, Kennedy delivered three special messages to Congress on federal aid to education.

However, because of his lack of success in obtaining federal aid to education, neither the biographies nor memoirs of his aides dwell on the issue. Kennedy's chief speech writer, Theodore Sorenson, barely mentions education in his early 800-page memoirs. Neither does Arthur Schlesinger, Jr., Kennedy's intellectual-in-resident, dwell on education in his more than 1,000-page memoirs. These historians have concentrated on Kennedy's dealings in foreign affairs.

One of the reasons Kennedy was unsuccessful in the passage of a federal aid to education bill was the nature of that proposal. Kennedy mainly repackaged older versions of federal aid bills to give monies for school construction and the raising of teacher salaries. Such items were not designed to obviate the opposition of religious groups, especially the Catholic church, which wanted any aid to include them. By Johnson's attempt in 1965, the focus was brilliantly shifted to aiding the child—a concept that skirted the constitutional issue of church and state. Another reason Kennedy lacked success in this area was his weak relations with Congress. Kennedy had neither the temperament to persuade Congress nor the status of a congressional "insider" that Lyndon Johnson enjoyed.

Nevertheless, Kennedy kept up a bully pulpit on education. Education was a prominent theme in the 1960 presidential campaign, State of the Union messages and press conferences. Most importantly, Kennedy delivered three special messages to Congress with federal aid to education plans. Education had become such a prominent feature of the New Frontier that he planned to make it a major campaign issue in 1964.[106]

Still, Kennedy was essentially a cold warrior. His acceptance speech at the 1960 Democratic party convention rings with cold war rhetoric. He asked "Can a nation organized and governed such as ours endure?"[107] This was the ultimate "question of the New Frontier."[108]

In his inaugural speech, Kennedy gave eloquent tribute to the cold war mentality. He proclaimed America's military readiness: "Let every nation know, whether it wishes us well or ill, that we shall pay any price, bear any burden, meet any hardship, support any friend, oppose any foe to assure the survival and the success of liberty."[109]

An important subtheme to the inaugural speech was poverty. Kennedy optimistically declared that "man holds in his mortal hands the power to abolish all forms of human poverty and all forms of human life."[110] Kennedy's faith in the ability of government to abolish poverty reflected the liberal optimism of the time. He presaged the rediscovery of mass poverty by Michael Harrington in his polemic *The Other America*.

For Kennedy, the cold war gave added meaning to strengthening education. In the 1960 presidential campaign, he declared that "education is the key to our future."[111] In his third special message on education to Congress in 1963, he continued linking education to the cold war. "Education," he proclaimed, "is the keystone in the area of freedom and progress."[112]

In his first State of the Union message, Kennedy emphasized the cold war, the recession and education. He repeated that the question remained whether "a nation organized and governed such as ours can endure."[113] For Kennedy, "the outcome is by no means certain."[114]

Kennedy found the economy's health "disturbing."[115] He foreshadowed an eventual poverty program by observing that "our cities are being engulfed by squalor" and that some 23 million Americans were "living in substandard homes."[116]

Kennedy reflected previous thinking on education in this message. He echoed the need for school construction and qualified teachers. According to Kennedy, American classrooms were overloaded with some 2 million children more than "they can properly have room for taught by 90,000 teachers not properly qualified to teach."[117] Moreover, the poor were unable to attend college. Kennedy estimated that fully "one-third of our most promising graduates are financially unable to continue the developments of their talents."[118] Still, Kennedy, the cold warrior, concluded that "all these problems pale when placed beside those which confront us around the world."[119]

By 1962, the State of the Union message shifted mostly to the domestic front. Education received more attention. Kennedy argued that "equally important to our strength is the quality of our education."[120] He mentioned his first federal aid to education bill, which he would send to Congress, for school construction and teacher salaries. He focused on the problem of illiteracy, that "eight million adult Americans are classified as functionally illiterate."[121] He returned to the theme of aiding the poor in attending college. "If this nation is to grow in wisdom and strength," he said, "then every able-bodied high school graduate should have the opportunity to develop his talents."[122] Yet, according to Kennedy, many "lack either the funds or the facilities to attend college."[123]

In Kennedy's last State of the Union message in 1963, the concern with education grew even stronger. He proposed educational measures that were rooted in "a series of fundamental premises."[124] First among these was "the need to strengthen our nation by investing in our youth."[125] He reiterated the damage to our country's "future" when students are "not educated to the fullest capacity from grade school to graduate school."[126] He estimated that four of every ten students in the fifth grade "will not even finish high school—and that is a waste we cannot afford."[127]

Kennedy gave three special messages to Congress on education in each of his three years in office. His program was threefold: (1) raise teacher salaries; (2) embark on school construction; and (3) provide scholarships for the needy to attend college. One commentator described the Kennedy program as "the most ambitious educational program submitted by any President" up to that time.[128]

Kennedy made a strong plea for aid to the deserving poor to attend college; "no task before our nation is more important."[129] "The concept that every American deserves the opportunity to attain the highest level of education of which he is capable," he declared," is a traditional ideal of democracy."[130]

Although Kennedy failed to enact any of his educational ideas, he maintained a steady drumbeat for federal aid to education. Moreover, he evinced concern for higher education of the poor. In short, Kennedy laid the groundwork for Lyndon Johnson's Great Society. (Lyndon B. Johnson's accomplishments will be fully discussed in chapter 4.)

RICHARD NIXON (1969–1974) AND GERALD FORD (1974–1977) AND THE POLITICS OF MAINTENANCE

President Richard Nixon offered little innovative departures in education from his predecessor Lyndon B. Johnson. For the most part, he continued Great Society educational programs with their emphasis on the education of the poor. Neither did Nixon's successor, Gerald Ford offer new ideas.

Nixon had been an excellent student and enjoyed his education. His most sympathetic biographer, Stephen Ambrose, described Nixon's California high school experience as one in which he was a top student "serious about his work, eager to learn."[131] This attitude and hard work ethic carried over to his college years at Whittier, a 400-student Quaker college; he graduated second in his class, having been in the honor society four years. Ambrose perceived Nixon as a student "close to the ideal," being "extremely intelligent, quick to learn, polite, a hard worker who did his homework and then some."[132] As a result Nixon received a scholarship to Duke University Law School.

Still, Nixon was not an education-minded president. One of his aides, Chester E. Finn, Jr., estimated that Nixon devoted but a scant six hours to educational issues in the first two years of his presidency.[133] His main interest was foreign affairs.

As a scholarship student, however, Nixon could understand the plight of able students who needed assistance for their academic pursuits. He continued Johnson's emphasis on aiding the poor in education. He declared in his message on education to Congress in 1970 that "for most of our citizens, the American educational system is among the most successful in the history of the world."[134] But for the poor, Nixon added, "it has never delivered on its promises."[135]

Nixon's answer was to strengthen the college loan program for the needy. He told Congress that "no qualified student who wants to go to college should be barred by lack of money."[136] Consequently, he sought to "revamp aid" to emphasize "helping low income students."[137]

Still, Nixon was an educational conservative. He subscribed to the emergent theory that schools had little positive effect on student achievement. This theory held that one's socioeconomic background and family influence held the greatest sway. Nixon declared that "most education takes place outside the school."[138]

This view received its greatest support from the massive government study, *Equality of Educational Opportunity*. The study was commissioned under the Johnson administration and popularly known as the Coleman report after its chief author, James Coleman. Published in 1966, the Coleman study slowly filtered into the public consciousness. Christopher Jencks and his associates at Harvard re-examined the data and reached the same conclusions in 1973.

Coleman and his associates concluded that the most predictable variable to school achievement was family background. They found, among their sample of 645,000 schoolchildren nationwide, that resources had little effect on student achievement. Few criticized the Coleman study. But those demurrers were spurred on to their own research, using different methodology. By the late 1970s, this research, known as the effective school movement, found some schools to have had dramatic impact on the poor in terms of student achievement. But the nihilism of the Coleman study influenced the Nixon-Ford administrations in failing to offer bold new programs in education.

The one new idea was a federal research agency. In his message on education "reform" in 1970, Nixon created the National Institute of Education (NIE) to encourage and direct research in education. Nixon's rationale was that "we must stop pretending that we understand the mystery of the learning process."[139] For Nixon the NIE would be "the first step toward reform."[140] A decade and a half later, the Reagan administration declared that one now knew what worked in education and dismantled NIE.

Appraisals of the Nixon presidency regarding education varied. Nixon aides such as Daniel Patrick Moynihan ranked the Nixon efforts with the great innovative thrusts by former presidents as constituting a "coming of age of education policy as an aspect of national social policy."[141] Neoconservative historians such as Diane Ravitch viewed Nixon's experimental schools plan as "one of the most ambitious federal efforts to reform the schools," despite the fact that they produced negligible results.[142]

Others perceived Nixon's efforts as a "great retreat." Revisionist historian

Joel Spring criticized Nixon's vetoes on federal spending bills on education as evidence of Nixon's lackluster interest in the subject. Spring contended that Nixon justified the vetoes on the spurious grounds of balancing the budget and Nixon's belief, based on the Coleman report, that there was a "lack of evidence that improved schooling resulted in any significant change."[143]

In the short two years in which Gerald Ford finished the Nixon presidency, he also failed to offer a fresh vision of education. Nevertheless, he paid lip service to the concept of education on the national agenda.

Ford was not especially keen on education. Despite financial difficulties, he attended the University of Michigan, where he received a full year's "bookstore" scholarship prior to attending, waited on tables, and obtained some pocket money from relatives. Reflecting in his memoirs on his college experience, he spoke almost wholly of his football-playing experience. Somewhat ruefully, he mused that if he were to return to college "knowing what I know today," he would concentrate on "learning to write and to speak before an audience."[144] As a public figure, he was deficient in both areas.

Still, he emphasized the need for a concern for education. He argued that "in the past decade America's problems have been national in scope."[145] He described the federal government's "encouragement and assistance to education" as an "essential part of the American system."[146]

Despite the national interest in education, Ford believed that education was primarily a state responsibility. He declared that "our Founding Fathers ... clearly saw education as a State responsibility."[147] The role of the federal government, he argued, was not to "usurp the state and local role."[148]

Nevertheless, he maintained the federal government's leadership established by Johnson on the education of the poor. His administration concentrated its monies on the "needs of the handicapped and the educationally deprived."[149]

Both Nixon and Ford had been students who were not financially well off and who had been able to attend schools because of scholarships and part-time work. As presidents, they extended the concept of aiding the poor through federal programs begun by Johnson. Yet their political philosophies were rooted in a conservative ideology that limited their views of universal education. Most importantly, they subscribed to the prevailing dogma that family influences, rather than the impact of the school, were the key to student achievement. Nevertheless, they continued the tradition of national concern for education that had started with Roosevelt, but theirs was an educational politics of maintenance.

JIMMY CARTER (1977–1981) AND THE DEPARTMENT OF EDUCATION

Jimmy Carter continued the national presence in education. Most significantly, Carter created a separate Department of Education. This accomplishment was at the urging of the largest teacher union, the National Education Association (NEA).

For the most part, Carter did not place education as a major priority in his presidency. He had attended the naval academy and had been a successful farmer. His strongest influence did not come from any teacher. Carter regarded his superior, Admiral Hyman Rickover, with whom he worked on the development of the atomic submarine, as his chief influence. Rickover, Carter wrote, "had a profound effect on my life—perhaps more than anyone except my parents."[150] Nevertheless, Carter inherited few of Rickover's educational ideas. Perhaps the only Rickover-influenced idea was a call for national testing—a position successfully opposed in presidential councils by the NEA, Secretary of Health, Education and Welfare Joseph Califano, and some national educators.[151]

Carter's main campaign goals were to restore trust in government in the wake of the Watergate scandal and to pare down the federal bureaucracy. In his campaign biography, Carter argued that a president "must give top priority to a drastic and thorough revision of the federal bureaucracy."[152] He based his credentials for that post on his streamlining Georgia state government while governor from 300 state agencies to 22.[153]

For a Democrat, Carter's political philosophy edged toward the conservative. Carter lectured Congress in his 1978 State of the Union message that "government cannot solve our problems."[154] He believed that "government cannot eliminate poverty or provide a bountiful economy or reduce inflation, or save our cities, or cure illiteracy, or provide energy."[155]

Although education was not a major policy issue, Carter was proeducation to a large extent. He increased the federal aid established by Lyndon Johnson—doubling the percentage of nondefense dollars spent on education.[156] Most importantly, he perceived himself as an advocate for education. Carter claimed to have entered state politics because he was primarily "concerned about the threats to our system of education" after having served on his county school board.[157] He cited in his memoirs "as one of my strongest convictions" that "every academically qualified student should have the opportunity to attend college."[158]

Carter's main achievement in education was the creation of a Department of Education. In this respect, he was merely following the wishes of one of his chief presidential supporters, the NEA, which had become a dominant political force in state and local elections. By 1976, the organization decided to support a presidential candidate for the first time.

The NEA had two national priorities in education. First, it sought the creation of a Department of Education. Education had traditionally been an "office," originally designed to collect statistics, in the Department of Health, Education and Welfare. NEA officials believed a separate cabinet department would confer upon education greater national importance. NEA officials pointed out that every major nation, except the United States, has departments or ministries of education.

In addition, the NEA desired a stronger federal role in education. From the early 1970s the NEA sought to expand federal expenditures from a high of 9 percent of the national education cost to as much as 33.3 percent. For the NEA, education was a national concern and responsibility.

Accordingly, the NEA made the Department of Education a condition of its presidential support. In the primaries Jimmy Carter declared to the NEA that he "was in favor of creating a separate Cabinet-level Department of Education" although "generally" he was "opposed to the proliferation of federal agencies."[159] Carter reasoned that a new education department would result in a "stronger voice for education at the federal level."[160]

There is some evidence that Carter wavered on the issue after the election.[161] Critics maintained that only the thought of re-election and the fear of losing NEA support made him push on with the department. Certainly, Carter muted his support. In his 1978 State of the Union message, he mentioned the creation of a new education department in only one sentence—after five paragraphs summarizing his success in streamlining the federal bureaucracy.

The call for another department read as follows: "And now it's time to take another step by creating a separate department of education."[162] Still, in his memoirs Carter rationalized his support; he claimed that the new department was better for policy delivery and had "lower administrative costs and fewer employees."[163]

The NEA stood nearly alone on this issue. A large segment of the liberal, labor and civil rights groups was opposed. A strong critic of the proposed Department of Education was teacher union rival, Albert Shanker, president of the American Federation of Teachers, AFL-CIO. Shanker lambasted the idea as adding another bureaucratic layer to education mainly for the reason of "prestige," which he felt was "not a good reason."[164] Others perceived Shanker's opposition on the grounds that he feared the NEA would dominate a new education department.[165]

An equally strong critic of the department was Carter's own secretary of Health, Education and Welfare, Joseph Califano. Califano subscribed to the belief that the federal government's role in education should be severely limited and that the chief function of the federal government in education should be primarily "to provide access to education."[166] He believed that a separate Department of Education would constitute "a fundamental change in that role."[167]

The strongest administration supporter for a new department was Vice-President Walter Mondale. Mondale had a deep concern in education in his years as a U.S. senator. Along with NEA officials, he was able to persuade Carter to keep his campaign promise. Califano maintained that Carter's renewed support was "largely political in terms of his own renomination and re-election."[168]

The measure was not a foregone conclusion. Opponents waged a bitter fight, raising diversionary issues such as busing and school prayer.[169] Only strong lobbying by the president and the NEA gained a narrow victory. In the House of Representatives, the government operations committee voted the bill to the main floor by the margin of four votes. The Senate victory was more substantial: seventy-two to twenty-one.[170] In time opponents of the department, such as Shanker and President Ronald Reagan, perceived the value of the new department.

In sum, Jimmy Carter extended the national concern with education. He extended Great Society programs and, most importantly, was responsible for the creation of the U.S. Department of Education in 1979. In turn, the department has been a significant arm of the presidency throughout the 1980s in exerting crucial influence nationally in education.

CONCLUSION

After World War II, eduation became a national issue as the United States emerged as a world power. However, few presidents came to the White House with a prepared educational agenda. They responded to national education concerns as they arose.

Moreover, presidents acted from their own political philosophies of government. Democrats were more prone than Republicans to perceive education as a key social issue arguing for spending programs. For the most part, Republican presidents were more likely than Democratic presidents to be fiscally prudent, viewing education on an accounting ledger.

In addition, presidents varied in their educational philosophies. At one end of the spectrum, Eisenhower saw only an "emergency role" for the federal government. At the other end of the spectrum, Lyndon Johnson believed that the federal government should have a proactive leadership role in education.

NOTES

1. John Kenneth Galbraith, *The Affluent Society* (Boston: Houghton Mifflin, 1958), p. 5.

2. Ibid., p. 86.

3. Ibid., p. 96.

4. Ibid., p. 100.

5. Daniel Bell, *The Coming of Post-Industrial Society* (New York: Basic Books, 1973), p. 134.

6. Ibid., pp. 129-30.

7. Ibid., p. 134.

8. Ibid., p. 143.

9. Ibid., p. 232.

10. Lester C. Thurow, *The Zero-Sum Society* (New York: Penguin Books, 1981), p. 82.

11. Ibid., p. 11.

12. Ibid., p. 5.

13. Ibid., p. 3.

14. Ibid., p. 46.

15. Diane Ravitch, *The Troubled Crusade: American Education, 1945-1980* (New York: Basic Books, 1983), pp. 10-18.

16. George A. Kizer, "Federal Aid to Education 1945-1963," *History of Education Quarterly,* Spring 1970.

17. Ted Morgan, *FDR: A Biography* (New York: Simon and Schuster, 1985).

18. Samuel I. Rosenman, ed., *The Public Papers and Addresses of Franklin D. Roosevelt,* vol. 11 (New York: Russell and Russell, 1950), p. 53.

19. Ibid., p. 54.

20. Ibid.

21. Ibid.

22. Ibid.

23. Ravitch, *The Troubled Crusade,* p. 15.

24. Gail Kennedy, ed., *Education for Democracy* (Boston: D.C. Heath, 1952), p. 8.

25. Ibid.

26. Ibid.

27. Ravitch, *The Troubled Crusade,* p. 17.

28. Ibid.

29. Maurice R. Berube, *The Urban University in America* (Westport, Conn.: Greenwood Press, 1978), p. 119.

30. Ibid., p. 103.

31. E. Edmund Reutter, Jr., and Robert R. Hamilton, eds., *The Law of Public Education,* 2d ed. (Mineola, N.Y.: Foundation Press, 1976), p. 220.

32. Ibid.

33. Kennedy, *Education for Democracy,* p. 8.

34. Ibid., p. 1.

35. Keith W. Olson, *The G.I. Bill, the Veterans and the Colleges* (Lexington: University Press of Kentucky, 1974), p. 3.

36. Franklin Delano Roosevelt, "Message to Congress," *New York Times,* November 24, 1943, p. 11.

37. Harry S Truman, "State of the Union Message," *New York Times,* September 7, 1945, p. 16.

38. Ibid.

39. Harry S Truman, "State of the Union Message," *New York Times,* January 6, 1946, p. 2.

40. Harry S Truman, "State of the Union Message," *New York Times,* January 7, 1947, p. 16.

41. Ibid.

42. Olson, *The G.I. Bill,* p. 5.

43. Rosenman, *Public Papers and Addresses of Franklin D. Roosevelt,* p. 470.

44. Olson, *The G.I. Bill,* p. 19.

45. Kennedy, *Education for Democracy*, p. 8.

46. Olson, *The G.I. Bill*, p. 143.

47. Ibid., p. 29.

48. Ibid., p. 33.

49. Ibid.

50. Ibid.

51. Ibid., p. 51.

52. Ibid., p. 49.

53. Donald R. McCoy, *The Presidency of Harry S. Truman* (Lawrence: University Press of Kansas, 1984).

54. Ibid., p. 37.

55. Harry S Truman, *Years of Trial and Hope 1946-1952* (Garden City, N.Y.: Doubleday, 1956), p. 207.

56. *Public Papers of the Presidents of the United States: Harry S. Truman, 1949* (Washington, D.C.: U.S. Government Printing Office, 1946), p. 167.

57. Ibid.

58. *Public Papers of the Presidents of the United States: Harry S. Truman* (Washington, D.C.: U.S. Government Printing Office, 1965), p. 94.

59. Dwight D. Eisenhower, *Waging Peace* (Garden City, N.Y.: Doubleday, 1965).

60. Dwight D. Eisenhower, "Press Conference," *New York Times*, October 31, 1957, p. 10.

61. Robert F. Burk, *Dwight D. Eisenhower: Hero and Politician* (Boston: Twayne, 1986), p. 104.

62. Dwight D. Eisenhower, "Education Message to Congress," *New York Times,* January 28, 1958, p. 18.

63. Ibid.

64. *New York Times*, October 6, 1957, p. 42.

65. *New York Times*, November 17, 1957, p. 8.

66. Ibid.

67. Ibid.

68. *New York Times*, December 6, 1957, p. 8.

69. *New York Times*, November 11, 1957, p. 11.

70. Ibid.

71. *New York Times*, December 6, 1957, p. 8.

72. *New York Times*, November 12, 1957, p. 24.

73. *New York Times*, November 3, 1957, p. 20.

74. David Marden Lane, "The Cold War and American Education," Ph.D. diss., University of Michigan, October 1957, p. 2.

75. *New York Times*, November 14, 1957, p. 27.

76. Ravitch, *The Troubled Crusade*, p. 51.

77. Hyman G. Rickover, *Education and Freedom* (New York: E.P. Dutton, 1959), p. 15.

78. Ibid., p. 136.

79. Ibid., p. 189.

80. Ibid.

81. *New York Times*, November 25, 1957, p. 17.

82. The American Assembly, *Goals for Americans* (New York: Prentice-Hall, 1960), p. 3.

83. The Rockefeller Panel, *Prospects for America* (Garden City, N.Y.: Doubleday, 1961), p. 25.

84. Ibid., p. 349.

85. American Assembly, *Goals for Americans,* p. 6.

86. Eisenhower, *Waging Peace,* p. 205.

87. Eisenhower, "Press Conference," p. 10.

88. Eisenhower, *Waging Peace,* p. 216.

89. Barbara Barksdale Clowse, *Brainpower for the Cold War: The Sputnik Crisis and the National Defense Education Act of 1958* (Westport, Conn.: Greenwood Press, 1981), p. 153.

90. Ibid.

91. Ibid.

92. Ibid., p. 162.

93. Ibid.

94. Ibid., pp. 163-64.

95. *Congressional Record,* Eighty-fifth Congress, 2d Session, vol. 104 (Washington, D.C.: U.S. Government Printing Office, 1958), p. 17,230.

96. Ibid., p. 17,231.

97. Ibid., p. 17,235.

98. Clowse, *Brainpower for the Cold War,* p. 117.

99. Ibid., p. 155.

100. Stephen E. Ambrose, *Eisenhower: The President,* vol. 2 (New York: Simon and Schuster), p. 460.

101. Ibid.

102. William T. O'Hara, *John F. Kennedy on Education* (New York: Teachers College Press, 1966), p. 24.

103. James MacGregor Burns, *John F. Kennedy: A Political Profile* (New York: Harcourt Brace, 1959), p. 162.

104. Paul Charles Light, *President's Agenda: Domestic Policy Choice from Kennedy to Carter* (Baltimore: Johns Hopkins University Press, 1982), p. 70.

105. Ibid.

106. O'Hara, *John F. Kennedy on Education,* p. 1.

107. John F. Kennedy, "Acceptance Speech—Democratic National Convention," *New York Times,* July 16, 1960, p. 7.

108. Ibid.

109. John F. Kennedy, "Inaugural Address," *New York Times,* January 21, 1961, p. 8.

110. Ibid.

111. O'Hara, *John F. Kennedy on Education,* p. 83.

112. Ibid., p. 154.

113. John F. Kennedy, "State of the Union Message," *New York Times,* January 12, 1961, p. 8.

114. Ibid.

115. Ibid.

116. Ibid.

117. Ibid.

118. Ibid.

119. Ibid.

120. Kennedy, "State of the Union Message," p. 12.

121. Ibid.

122. Ibid.

123. Ibid.

124. John F. Kennedy, "State of the Union Message," *New York Times* (Western edition), January 15, 1963, p. 4.

125. Ibid.

126. Ibid.

127. Ibid.

128. O'Hara, *John F. Kennedy on Education*, p. 25.

129. Ibid., p. 133.

130. Ibid.

131. Stephen E. Ambrose, *Nixon: The Education of a Politician, 1913-1962* (New York: Simon and Schuster, 1987), p. 49.

132. Ibid., p. 58.

133. George R. Kaplan, "Hail to a Chief or Two: The Indifferent Presidential Record in Education," *Phi Delta Kappan,* September 1984, p. 10.

134. Richard M. Nixon, "Message on Education Reform," *American Education,* April 1970, p. 34.

135. Ibid.

136. Richard M. Nixon, "Special Message to the Congress on Higher Education—March 19, 1970," in *Education and the Presidency,* ed. Chester Finn, Jr. (Lexington, Mass.: Lexington Books, 1977), p. 133.

137. Ibid.

138. Nixon, "Message on Education Reform," p. 32.

139. Ibid., p. 30.

140. Ibid.

141. Finn, *Education and the Presidency*, p. x.

142. Ravitch, *The Troubled Crusade,* p. 258.

143. Joel Spring, *The Sorting Machine Revisited: National Educational Policy Since 1945* (New York: Longman, 1989), p. 164.

144. Gerald R. Ford, *A Time to Heal* (New York: Harper and Row, 1979), p. 50.

145. Gerald R. Ford, "My Vision of Education," *American Education,* April 1976, p. 14.

146. Ibid.

147. Ibid.

148. Ibid.

149. Ibid.

150. Jimmy Carter, *Why Not the Best?* (Nashville, Tenn.: Broad Press, 1975), p. 57.

151. Joseph A. Califano, Jr., *Governing America* (New York: Simon and Schuster, 1981), p. 298.

152. Carter, *Why Not the Best?,* p. 147.

153. Ibid., p. 112.

154. Jimmy Carter, "State of the Union Message," *New York Times,* January 20, 1978, p. 12.

155. Ibid.

156. Jimmy Carter, *Keeping Faith: Memoirs of a President* (New York: Bantam Books, 1982), p. 75.

157. Ibid.

158. Ibid.

159. Califano, *Governing America,* p. 274.

160. Ibid.

161. Ibid., p. 293.

162. Carter, "State of the Union Message, 1978," p. 12.

163. Carter, *Keeping the Faith,* p. 76.

164. Albert Shanker, "No Reason for Separate Education Department," *New York Times,* March 4, 1979, p. E.7.

165. Califano, *Governing America,* p. 279.

166. Ibid.

167. Ibid., p. 293.

168. Ibid.

169. Maurice R. Berube, *Teacher Poiltics: The Influence of Unions* (Westport, Conn.: Greenwood Press, 1988), p. 24.

170. Califano, *Governing America,* p. 285.

4

Lyndon B. Johnson (1963–1969) and the Equity Reform Movement

Lyndon B. Johnson was the ultimate education president. He coined the phrase to describe himself. Moreover, he was an education president by design, and not by accident as was the case with Ronald Reagan.

For Johnson, education was the key ingredient of his Great Society. He promoted education both through a bully pulpit and with substantive education programs.

Johnson wanted to be remembered in history chiefly as the education president. He could point to over sixty education bills signed into law during his tenure—including the historic first federal aid to education act. He wanted to be known as the president "who wants our era remembered as the education era."[1] Some critics considered that statement to be an afterthought. However, his vice-president, Hubert Humphrey, contended that Johnson wanted to be known for his efforts on behalf of education from the earliest days of his tenure.[2]

Actually, Johnson inherited his national agenda from President John F. Kennedy. Kennedy had set the parameters of his administration on a federal aid to education bill and a poverty program, but he had been unable to fulfill that agenda. It was left to Johnson, a more able administrator, to do so. He acknowledged the debt in his memoirs: "Rightly or wrongly, I felt from the very first day in office that I had to carry on for President Kennedy. I considered myself the caretaker of both his people and his policies."[3]

The Kennedy agenda suited Johnson well. He tended to romanticize his early poverty and his experience as a schoolteacher; consequently, he was extremely sympathetic to the cause of public education. He modeled himself after Franklin D. Roosevelt and was an old-line Southern Rooseveltian liberal. He responded to the urgent domestic demands of his era with a combination of liberal ideology and political pragmatism.

The major domestic event of Johnson's time was the civil rights movement. It was an idea whose time had come, and Johnson reversed his conservative Southern prejudices to help enact major civil rights laws. Concomitantly, mass poverty was rediscovered during the early 1960s; consequently, poverty and civil rights were to blend together.

The civil rights movement spurred an educational reform movement— "equity reform"—that emphasized the education of the poor. This contrasts sharply with the second major reform movement in the 1980s—"excellence reform," sponsored by the Reagan administration—that emphasized the other end of the spectrum: the education of the best and brightest in order to compete with foreign economic powers.

Johnson was clear on the importance education held in his vision of America. Six months after the assassination of President Kennedy, he announced his plans for a Great Society, in which education had a most prominent place. He declared:

We have the opportunity to move not only toward the rich society, but upward to the Great Society....

So I want to talk to you today about the three places where we begin to build the Great Society—in our cities, in our countryside, and in our classrooms.... These are the three central issues of the Great Society.[4]

What comprised the Great Society? Essentially, Johnson wove a comprehensive set of innovative programs that addressed the problem of poverty and the concerns of the civil rights movement. These programs were chiefly in three areas: education, social welfare and civil rights.

In education, the major accomplishments fell into three categories. First, Johnson scored a breakthrough with the first federal aid to education bill; second, he followed with a higher education act; and third, he incorporated preschool education for the children of the poor—Head Start—in his poverty program.

In social welfare, Johnson's major accomplishments were in health. He drafted and helped pass the first federal health program for the elderly— Medicare—and the poor—Medicaid.

In the area of civil rights, the Johnson administration was responsible for major civil rights legislation. For blacks and other minorities, the Civil Rights Act of 1964 guaranteed access to accommodations, employment and education opportunities. The Voting Rights Act of 1965 finally gave them the right to vote, which had been denied them in the South through various subterfuges.

The Great Society was mainly a response to the civil rights movement, and the major educational reform movement of the 1960s was a direct response to the black rights movement. A thesis of this study is that the two major educational reform movements—the equity reform movement of the 1960s and the excellence reform movement of the 1980s—were a result of outside societal pressures. They did not emerge from within the educational establishment.

Concomitantly, the larger social revolution of the Great Society was, in turn, a response to civil rights and the attention to poverty. Had there not been any Montgomeries or Selmas, it is hardly conceivable that civil rights legislation would have been enacted or an attack on poverty waged. Johnson's vision lay in responding to the major demands of his time.

Johnson, ever the political pragmatist, realized the precariousness of responding to moral and politically difficult mandates. There was an urgent political time clock on achieving the Great Society. He told aides that "we've got to do this in a hurry" because "we got in with this majority in Congress" and "we're going to lose them at a rate of a million a month."[5] Johnson realized that "every day while I'm in office I'm going to alienate somebody" and "it's going to be something" whether "it's going to be Vietnam or it's going to be this or that."[6] Consequently, he urged his aides to "get it during my honeymoon."[7]

JOHNSON AND EDUCATION

For Johnson, education was both a means to an end and an end in itself. His press secretary, George Reedy, recalled, in somewhat bitter memoirs, Johnson's obsession with education:

Nothing was in his thoughts more often. He sought guarantees that every boy or girl in the United States "could have all the education he or she can take." He was actually superstitious about the subject, and at times one expected him to advocate college as a cure for dandruff or university as a specific for sore throats.[8]

Other aides were also convinced of Johnson's love of education. His first commissioner of education, Francis Keppel, inherited from the Kennedy administration, recalled the difference between Kennedy and Johnson on education. When Kennedy's first commissioner of education, Sterling McMurrin, resigned through notifying not the president but his congressman, Kennedy was enraged that he learned of it through the newspapers. He replied in rage to his aide McGeorge Bundy, "What's going on. I never heard of this fellow."[9] Bundy replied, "That's exactly the trouble [because] you never heard of this fellow."[10]

By contrast, Johnson knew his education people well. Keppel recalled that "education was one of his real interests—genuine interests" and that "this isn't phony"; it was a "perfectly genuine interest."[11] Consequently, Keppel was invited to the White House socially.

His chief idea man and coordinator of legislative relations, Douglass Cater, corroborated this impression of Johnson. He recalled that Johnson's interest in education was "very genuine" and that he was "always urging me to bigger and bolder ideas in the education field."[12]

THE CIVIL RIGHTS MOVEMENT

The civil rights movement was the great social and political revolution of the 1960s. It affected every area of American life, especially the nature of education reform, and Lyndon Johnson responded to its challenge by undergoing a sea change in racial attitudes. From a conservative Southern liberal in race relations, he became a champion for the rights of blacks.

Civil rights was an idea whose time had come. Unlike John F. Kennedy, who tried to postpone that day, Johnson reacted swiftly and forcefully. Still, it was the pressure of the civil rights movement demonstrating in the streets of the South that helped convert Johnson to its cause. Johnson's staff recalled that civil rights was the most discussed domestic issue after poverty—with 79 percent mentioning it in a survey. By contrast, only 18 percent of Kennedy staffers cited civil rights as a national priority, the last of five major items.[13] Arthur Schlesinger, Jr., observed that Kennedy "concluded that there was no possible chance of passing a civil rights bill ... and a fight for civil rights would alienate southern support he needed for other purposes."[14]

For Johnson it was a movement that would not fade. As a Southern politician of long standing in Congress, he enjoyed the status of being a member of the "club"—the inner circle whose clout he had accumulated. Consequently, he was able to pass programs through Congress with a success that Kennedy found difficult.

The civil rights movement underwent four main stages. First, it scored an important legal victory with the Supreme Court in 1954 in the *Brown* decision, which mandated school integration. The *Brown* decision had, in turn, three major impacts: (1) civil rights was a federal concern; (2) education was defined as a major goal of the black rights movement; and (3) the victory by the National Association for the Advancement of Colored People (NAACP) set the stage for a mass movement that would employ the pressure tactics of demonstrations.

The second stage was mass demonstrations, which were keyed initially to obtain equal access to accommodations and later to obtain educational opportunities and voting rights. These demonstrations supplemented the legal strategy of the NAACP, involved more people, and gave rise to emerging, dynamic young leadership in the black community based in the black church.

The third stage was the student sit-ins begun in 1960. The involvement of the young elite in the black community—college students—re-energized the civil rights movement and brought youth and new idealism to the cadre of civil rights activists.

The final stage was the Black Power movement in 1966, which has dominated civil rights to this day. Prior to the emergence of Black Power, the civil rights movement was essentially integrationist. Black Power refocused the movement into one emphasizing group solidarity and black identity.

Why did the civil rights movement succeed? For one thing, the demographics had changed. Southern agriculture had been dramatically altered with modernization so that blacks moved to the North and from rural areas to Southern cities. In 1900, 87 percent of the black population in the South were in agriculture or domestic service; by 1960 less than 10 percent were in agriculture and 15 percent in domestic service. In 1900, more than 90 percent of blacks lived in the South; by 1960, nearly 50 percent lived in the North.[15] And by 1960, Southern rural blacks had mostly moved to cities, thus enabling the black church to channel racial discontent within the matrix of a new urban mass.[16]

Moreover, as Frances Fox Piven and Richard Cloward argue, the civil rights movement was gaining new strength at a time when the rhetoric of freedom was incessantly proclaimed by the American government. In the fifties and sixties, the cold war had reached its height. America's ideological exportation of ideas of political freedom clashed with its treatment of blacks. The painful incongruity eventually caused an agonizing reappraisal within the hearts and minds of America's leaders.

Still, no change in white America's attitudes toward race would have come about without the constant pressure of the civil rights movement. The timing might have been ripe for change, but the push to change was needed.

Among the dynamic young leaders of the movement was the Reverend Dr. Martin Luther King, Jr. King was the son of a minister in an important Atlanta church and had received a doctorate in theology from Boston University. Somewhat like Lyndon Johnson, he was an "accidental" leader, having been thrust into the leadership of the Montgomery bus boycott because of his lack of enemies within the black and white communities. Although young and inexperienced, he grew with the movement and dominated it. King influenced its nonviolent direction—a position he held as a disciple of Gandhi and Thoreau.

Lyndon Johnson reached out to his times. Before the emergence of the civil rights movement, Johnson had assiduously avoided identification with civil rights. He informed his official biographer, Doris Kearns, that he did not consider himself a Southern bigot but that "civil rights was not one of my priorities."[17] However, he was quick to add, "That all changed when I became President."[18]

For King, Johnson was at first an unknown on civil rights. King was hesitant to support him for president in 1964 until he could discern "how he acts in a crisis, like Kennedy."[19] Although they acted in tandem on civil rights, King distanced himself from Johnson over the Vietnam War, which he considered immoral.[20]

Johnson's support of civil rights came early as president. Five short days after the assassination of Kennedy, Johnson declared to Congress that for civil rights "it is time now . . . to write it in the book of law."[21] Kearns wrote that in rising to the occasion, Johnson "had become a moral leader."[22]

This declaration cost him votes. In the 1964 presidential election, he lost his white constituency in the Deep South, although he obtained 90 percent of the black vote. Aware of this eroding constituency, he pushed for civil rights and his Great Society with all deliberate speed.

By 1965, Johnson delivered his boldest proposal for alleviating the condition of blacks in America. In a commencement speech to the students at Howard University in Washington, D.C., Johnson moved beyond accommodation and voting to economic rights. He proclaimed that for blacks "just legal equity" was not enough.[23] What was required was "equality as a fact and equality as a result."[24] This meant decent jobs, housing, health care and incentives to repair the disintegrating black family. Most important was "a chance to learn—an equal chance to learn."[25] These goals were to be achieved through government programs. He ended his speech with a pledge: "And to all these fronts—and a dozen more—I will dedicate the expanding efforts of the Johnson administration."[26] It was an ambitious program, sincerely promised; however, Johnson was not to make good on his pledge. His growing obsession with a developing Vietnam War funneled both his attention and needed monies away from his Great Society for black America.

POVERTY

Poverty in America was rediscovered in the early 1960s by a number of scholars and journalists. Of the books published, Michael Harrington's *The Other America* did for poverty what Harriet Beecher Stowe's *Uncle Tom's Cabin* did for the abolition of slavery. *The Other America* defined a severe problem and galvanized the nation—more properly, the federal government—into action.

Prior to the publishing of Harrington's polemic in 1962, the official view was that there was little poverty still existing in the nation. This view was most succinctly expressed by the liberal economist John Kenneth Galbraith in *The Affluent Society,* published in 1958. Galbraith argued that "poverty is no longer a massive affliction [but] more nearly an afterthought."[27] He contended that only small isolated pockets of poverty—"case poverty"—remained in which the poor were primarily handicapped by physical or mental disabilities.

Harrington challenged that view. He convincingly presented a brief showing that at least 25 percent of Americans were poor. He defined poverty as that state in which people "are denied the minimal levels of health, housing, food, and education that our present stage of scientific knowledge specifies as necessary for life as it is lived in the United States."[28] By his calculations, 50 million of America's then population of some 200 million were poor.

One reason Americans such as Galbraith had not been aware of this massive poverty was that it was "invisible"—it "is often off the beaten track."[29] Rural slums were off the main highways built after World War II. Commuters on trains from the newly expanding suburbs would barely see the urban slums they drove through to work.

Despite being invisible, Harrington argued, poverty cut a wide swath in American society. Poverty was rural and urban, afflicting blacks and other minorities and the elderly. It was more than a lack of money; poverty took a psychological toll and crippled mentally.

The Other America overshadowed other reports on poverty published at that time for two major reasons. The lesser reason was that the book was immensely readable, a blend of journalism and scholarship, written with passion. The more important reason was that it caught the attention of two men. Dwight MacDonald, a former radical and contributor to the *New Yorker,* published a twenty-eight-page review of books on poverty that almost wholly dealt with *The Other America,* and John F. Kennedy, president of the United States, read the *New Yorker* review and then the book and found the modus vivendi for a major policy for his new administration.

MacDonald's review also included a review of two other books on poverty by scholarly economists, but he preferred Harrington's well-argued, impassioned account. Still, he saw the scholarly limitations of Harrington's polemic with its lack of footnotes, index and bibliography and its "treatment of statistics [as being] more than a little impressionistic."[30]

For the most part, reviewers of *The Other America* received it well; however, neither the reviewers nor Harrington anticipated its overwhelming impact. It was read by a president of the United States, and it served to fuel a national war on poverty. The *New York Times* labor reporter A.H. Raskin called the book a "stand-in for Dickens [written] with sensitivity and perception as well as indignation."[31] In a similar vein the *New York Herald Tribune* reviewer gently suggested that "it will go well for America if a good many of us read and take to heart Mr. Harrington's message."[32]

Perhaps the only negative note in the reception of *The Other America* came from my pen in an anonymous review for Kirkus, a prepublication agency serving libraries. In a review I wish I could now rewrite, I excessively enlarged on what Raskin was later to call "a stand-in for Dickens." I wrote:

The idea and scope of this book, on the face of it, is very promising. The reader is to be led on a journey through the economic subterranean world, overlooked in our conception of ourselves and neglected in print. But, somehow, despite the clear evidence of scholarship and breadth of imagination the journey becomes routine.

... The book is polemic yet it fails to point to causative factors. Moral indignation without direction is futile.... But *The Other America* does signal service, read as merely the casebook counterpart to the great unwritten novel of poverty.[33]

The mixed review stung Harrington. A generation later he wrote in his second autobiography:

I had written in *The Other America* that the American poor needed a Dickens to render the sight and smell and touch their misery and then I noted that I was not up to such a task. The anonymous critic at *Kirkus* thought my sad admission was one of the most persuasive parts of this book. On the whole, however, no one even laid a glove on me.[34]

Months after the reviews in the newspapers were printed, MacDonald's review was published. Kennedy read it and, later, Harrington's book and found an issue. In truth, he had long spoken of "pockets of poverty," in line with Galbraith's thesis, but the concept of massive poverty was new to him, and he was determined to fashion government policies to alleviate it.

The Other America was the right book for its time. Twenty-five years after its publication, a conservative Reagan aide observed that Harrington "published that book at the peak of the intellectual philosophy we think of as liberalism in the United States."[35] He added that he thought Harrington's views are "largely irrelevant today," in a conservative age.[36]

At the height of the 1960s liberalism, it was widely believed that government could solve major social problems. What was needed was a national will and financial resources to achieve those ends. Poverty, racism, war— all were thought to be capable of rational solution.

This politics of optimism concided with a flourishing economy. Unemployment was at a low 4 percent—which some economists would define as "realistic" full employment and contend that this number reflected mainly those who could not work because of disabilities. A young, buoyant John F. Kennedy revitalized government in the eyes of Americans and conveyed optimism to the young.

Consequently, for Harrington the solution to poverty was rather simple in 1962. What was needed was national will. He dramatically concluded *The Other America* with this challenge: "The means are at hand to fulfill the age-old dream: poverty can now be abolished. How long shall we ignore this underdeveloped nation in our midst? How long shall we look the other way while our fellow human beings suffer? How long?"[37]

By the 1980s, a conservative revolution crested with the election of the most conservative president of modern times. Policy analysts such as Edward Banfield, Nathan Glazer and Charles Murray argued that government was not capable of solving major social problems. They contended that these social problems were caused by family patterns, individual life-styles and personal choice—areas beyond the ken of social policy. Consequently, they argued, the individual's capacity or inability to plan for the future was the chief determination of poverty. This nihilism was reflected in Reagan administration policies.

By 1984, Harrington—under challenge from Murray—reassessed poverty. In *The New America Poverty,* he presented a more sober appraisal of the complexities of poverty. He contended that American poverty was now the victim of global economic forces; consequently, more than national will was involved in solving American poverty. Harrington concluded:

The poor are still there.

Two decades after the President of the United States declared an "unconditional" war on poverty, poverty does not simply continue to exist; worse, we must deal with *structures of misery,* with a new poverty *much more tenacious than the old.* . . .
The poor—and the entire American economy—are caught in a crisis that is *literally global.* . . . The great, *impersonal forces* have indeed created a context in which poverty is much more difficult to abolish than it was twenty-five years ago (emphasis added).[38]

Harrington's reappraisal was a reply to Murray's book of the same year, *Losing Ground.* For Murray, the best solution to poverty was prosperity. He repackaged the trickle-down theory, which maintained that in affluent times all segments of society profit. What happened between 1962 and 1984 was that poverty was no longer in fashion. "The poor receded from public attention," Murray wrote, until the Reagan administration viewed "social welfare programs [as] prime targets for budget cuts."[39]

Murray maintained that in the years after the Great Society, poverty remained at 13 percent of the population, even though "our expenditure on social welfare had quadrupled."[40] His explanation for that fact was that "the bright hopes of the sixties dimmed in the seventies as the economy slowed."[41] However, Murray did not sufficiently stress that Great Society programs reduced poverty from 30 percent to 13 percent of the American population.

AN AGE OF EDUCATIONAL REFORM

The 1960s were an era of educational reform. This reform movement, which shall be called the equity school reform movement, was a result of a combination of pressure from the civil rights movement and the reawakened interest in poverty. The equity reform movement focused on strategies to educate the poor, and the federal government under Lyndon Johnson responded with alacrity.

The civil rights movement set the direction of equity reform with its 1954

Supreme Court victory in *Brown* v. *Toledo, Kansas,* mandating school integration. The schools were a major target of civil rights activity to open up educational opportunities for blacks. By the sixties, civil rights groups were demanding the release of standardized test scores from big city school boards. The discovery of massive failure of poor blacks and other minorities shocked the nation.

Consequently, educators pressed for change. It was a heady time. New and exciting programs were proposed, and innovation was their theme. Reformers sought to change school governance, such as the community control movement (of which I was a part) for elected urban school boards with significant powers chosen by parents of public schoolchildren; other activitists pressed for school integration.

Publishers took advantage of this surge of interest. Education books were on a trade list—for the general public—and a plethora of exciting books was published. The popularity of education books was acknowledged by the choice of an education book in 1968 for the National Book Award in nonfiction. Jonathan Kozol's memoir of teaching in a Boston school, *Death at an Early Age,* became the only education book ever to achieve this status.

Educational scholarship followed suit. A golden age of educational history developed, of young, socially conscious Ph.Ds. This educational history, dubbed revisionism, examined our educational past and used new historical methods to understand our educating the poor. The revisionists concluded that America had never successfully accommodated itself to educating its poor.

Other forms of educational research also concentrated on the poor, and with a new flow of monies from Washington, educational research became more sophisticated.

The key idea of these equity reformers was that the failure in educating the poor was the responsibility of the schools. These romantic reformers assumed that the poor were educable. Consequently, it was the task of the schools to fashion teaching so that learning could take place among the poor.

That assumption came under severe challenge by the 1970s. One group of educational researchers concluded that educational achievement was dependent on socioeconomic background—what the child brought to the school.

The pendulum had swung back again by the early 1980s. Effective school researchers presented evidence that indicated that some schools were effective in teaching the poor. This optimism replaced the nihilism of the 1970s.

The Great Society, then, was not an isolated phenomenon. The Great Society rode in on a wave of widespread educational reform, itself a spin-off of the civil rights movement. It was an age of educational reform that was both energetic and optimistic.

THE JOHNSON EDUCATIONAL BULLY PULPIT

Lyndon Johnson used the bully pulpit to preach the message of education by means of major addresses, such as the inaugural address and State of the Union messages, as well as other speeches to the nation. Usually, Johnson tied in poverty with education. In his first four years, education was a major component of his addresses. By 1966, Vietnam emerged in the State of the Union message, and by 1968 it was a dominant theme.

Johnson staked out his educational contribution in his memoirs. He assessed that the crisis in education needed national direction, and he wrote that "educators and national leaders have been watching our great public school system become overwhelmed by the country's growing requirements."[42]

He perceived that federal aid was essential and concluded that "unless the federal government could step in and render necessary assistance many American children would be doomed to inferior education, which presaged an empty future."[43]

He made an educational pledge: "Because of these convictions, I made a personal decision during the 1964 campaign to make education a fundamental issue and to put it high on the nation's agenda."[44]

The 1964 Democratic party platform placed a high priority on education. It guaranteed college to anyone of ability despite personal inability to pay:

There can be full freedom only when all of our people have the opportunity for education to the full extent of their ability to learn, followed by the opportunity to employ their learning in the creation of something of value to themselves and the nation.

Our task is to make the national purpose serve the human purpose: that every person shall have the opportunity to become all that he or she is capable of becoming.

We believe that knowledge is essential to individual freedom and to the conduct of a free society. We believe that education is the surest and most profitable investment a nation can make.

Regardless of family financial status, therefore, education should be open to every boy and girl in America up to the highest level which he or she is able to master.[45]

On the other hand, the Republican party platform was more limiting; it urged "realistic spending in the most productive and creative areas, such as education."[46] The platform opposed a large federal role by "resisting Democratic efforts which endanger local control of schools."[47]

The Republican nominee, Arizona senator Barry Goldwater, spoke little of education in the campaign. He declared that he did not "believe we have an education problem which requires any form of Federal grant-in-aid program to the states."[48]

Poverty was woven into education early. In his first State of the Union message after the Kennedy assassination, Johnson declared "an unconditional war on poverty."[49] He singled out education as a key:

Our chief weapons in a more pinpointed attack will be better schools. Very often a lack of jobs and money is not the cause of poverty, but the symptom. The cause may lie deeper in our failure to give our fellow citizens a fair chance to develop their own capacities, in a lack of education and training.[50]

Education became a major campaign issue in 1964. His chief idea man, Douglass Cater, had "developed the firm conviction that the President ought to make education his top priority in his campaign."[51] Johnson agreed, and Cater "tried in various speeches...to stress this education priority."[52]

In his acceptance of the nomination Johnson asked his fellow Americans to "join me tonight in starting a program that will give every child education of the highest quality that he can take."[53] He reiterated the same theme in his inaugural address: "In a land of great wealth, families must not live in hopeless poverty.... In a great land of learning and scholars, young people must be taught to read and write."[54]

Johnson delivered a major address to Congress on education before the inauguration. His education message spelled out his strategy for federal aid. This message obviated the religious issue by proposing shared facilities, accomplished by targeting only poor children as recipients of aid—a "categorical" aid approach responding to a national issue rather than general aid.

Consequently, Johnson sounded the idea of national educational issues that demanded national policies:

I propose that we declare a national goal of full educational opportunity. Every child must be encouraged to get as much education as he has the ability to take. We want this not only for his sake—but for the nation's sake. Nothing matters more to the future of our country: not our military preparedness...not our productive economy...not our democratic system of government.[55]

Editorial writers at the *New York Times* applauded Johnson's "skillful effort to fix national priorities."[56] Indeed, the *Times* transcended Johnson's plea and recommended the creation of a cabinet post for education in light of Johnson's message, which "clearly demonstrates that education is of the highest concern."[57]

By 1966, Johnson continued the State of the Union message with an emphasis on domestic Great Society programs; education still was paramount. He asked Congress to "fulfill and improve the great health and education programs of last year."[58] But an escalating war in Vietnam made its first appearance. Johnson commented that "we can continue the Great Society while we fight in Vietnam" and thus touched off a guns-versus-butter debate.[59]

The same message was basically reiterated in the 1967 State of the Union message. He recommended that Congress "intensify our effort to give the poor a chance to enjoy and to join in this nation's progress."[60] He suggested this goal could be partially accomplished by adding a new program to Head Start, called Follow Through, which would extend gains made in the pre-school program to the first three years of regular school. He admitted that implementation problems of programs were largley due to innovation as the Great Society "set out to create new instruments of social progress."[61]

By 1968, Vietnam dominated the State of the Union message; the Great Society was shunted aside. Still, Johnson proposed "an educational opportunity act" that would enable the poor to attend college.[62]

JOHNSON AND THE INTELLECTUALS

Perhaps the cruelest irony was that the education president should be criticized by some leading scholars, intellectuals and artists. The dividing issue was Vietnam; many academics considered the Vietnam War immoral.

Johnson was not an intellectual. He had been a good schoolteacher and had an abiding faith in the curative powers of education, but he did not fit the stereotype of an intellectual. He was a hard-drinking, woman-chasing, coarse-speaking Southern "good old boy." His idea man, Douglass Cater, recalled that Johnson's favorite entertainment was "to talk, reminisce."[63] Unlike Kennedy, he did not have any cultural interests. His press secretary, George Reedy, remarked that Johnson "could not grasp intellectual disciplines."[64] Johnson "desired only the solutions to problems."[65] This personality, coupled with his growing obsession with Vietnam, led to "some very scratchy relationships with academicians."[66]

Realizing this weakness, Johnson appointed an "intellectual-in-residence," as had Kennedy. Johnson chose Princeton historian Eric Goldman. Vietnam was too difficult a hurdle even for the mild-mannered Goldman.

An example will illustrate Johnson's problems with the intellectual community. Goldman planned a White House Festival of the Arts for June 1965. Leading poets, novelists and artists were invited; the poet Robert Lowell was invited, and he accepted.

On reflection, Lowell reversed himself, declined the invitation and cited his opposition to the Vietnam War. He wrote the president that although he was very "enthusiastic about most of your domestic legislation and intentions," he could "only follow our present foreign policy with the greatest dismay and distrust."[67]

It was a cause célèbre. The *New York Times* reported the flap on its front page and caused Johnson to regard the placement of the story as further evidence of liberal hostility toward him over the war.[68]

By March, the academic community mobilized in protest over the war. The first of a nationwide series of teach-ins in opposition to the war took place at the University of Michigan at Ann Arbor. These teach-ins consisted of faculty lectures and seminars and spread quickly on college campuses from Maine to California.

In sum, the education president was reviled by an influential segment of the academic community.

JOHNSON'S EARLY INFLUENCES

Johnson's early familial influences were in politics and education. From his father, Sam Johnson, who was elected six times to the Texas legislature, he became predisposed to politics. From his mother, Rebekeh Johnson, a college graduate and schoolteacher, he received his interest in education.

Johnson was the oldest of five children. Although politics was to dominate his life, his mother and the world of culture she represented were what he remembered most fondly. According to biographer Doris Kearns, in the waning years of his life, Johnson "spoke almost exclusively of his mother."[69] His references to his father were generally negative.

Part of that resentment toward his father could be attributed to Sam Johnson's being a ne'er-do-well farmer. This status caused friction with his wife and later was partly responsible for a rebellious period in Lyndon's life when he refused to go to college and lived a marginal life in California for two years.

Johnson idealized his mother as "that sweet, gentle, cultured woman."[70] Some critics conceded Rebekeh's cultural interests but commented that they included pulp literature.[71] For George Reedy, Rebekeh was "a formidable woman with a sense of grievance" against her married fate.[72]

Johnson ended his rebellion in California and returned home. After a short period of cavorting with a local "wild bunch," he decided to attend college.[73]

Since money was scarce in the Johnson family, Lyndon attended San Marcos College, primarily a college for teacher preparation. He left for a year to teach public school in Cotulla, a poor Mexican community. Students remembered him as demanding but "in a way that made his students like him."[74]

Lyndon returned to college, graduated and embarked on a public school-teaching career. He taught in Pearsall and later for fifteen months in Houston; he taught in the speech department of a high school. He was remembered as "a teacher of such promise."[75] Finally, politics beckoned, and he became a congressional aide.

THE GREAT SOCIETY EDUCATIONAL PROGRAMS

Johnson inherited the concern over poverty and a federal aid to education bill. His particular genius was to exploit the favorable political winds of the time to have Congress approve those thrusts.

Kennedy had already begun formulating policies to ameliorate poverty. He had created a task force with his leading economic adviser, Walter Heller, as chairman. The major problem before the task force was which avenue to pursue: Should the poverty program concentrate on jobs and training or on education? The former strategy was advocated by Secretary of Labor Willard Wirtz and his assistant Daniel Patrick Moynihan. The latter strategy was put forth by economists Heller and Robert Lampman, among others.

For the economists, education was a key ingredient to a highly able work force and, concomitantly, economic prosperity. Heller concluded that "this acceptance of education is long overdue."[76] On the other hand, Moynihan iterated the labor point of view that "the most important measure that could be taken to combat poverty was more or less a massive employment program."[77]

For Johnson the solution was simple: emphasize education. He told the poverty policy analysts: "This is going to be an education program. We are going to eliminate poverty with education, and I don't want anybody ever to mention income redistribution . . . people are going to learn their way out of poverty" (paraphrased).[78]

This solution was consonant with Johnson's philosophy. Reedy observed that "at the heart of the matter was his conviction that education was the way out of poverty."[79] Indeed, according to Reedy, "the fundamental Johnsonian view of the universe was that of the rural 'po' boy' born to poverty and determined to exact vengeance from the aristocrats he regarded as holding him in contempt."[80] As president, he was interested in poverty and education. Reedy commented that "poverty, education, or economic opportunity [were] problems which really held his attention."[81]

Johnson also believed in consensus; consequently, the bill that was conceived and passed was a compromise. The Economic Opportunity Act 1964 had three main sections: education, job training and community action.

The education section was a bold new experiment in preschool for poor children. Called Head Start, it capitalized on recent early childhood research and became the most famous and successful of Great Society programs.

The second component was a job training program that also had some measure of success. One part involved a Neighborhood Youth Corps job program and the other a Job Corps, providing training at boarding schools.

The third component of the poverty bill proved most controversial. The community action program sought to enable the poor to participate in decision making. Community action was based on social science theories that the poor suffered more than a lack of money—they were alienated. Enabling them to participate politically, it was argued, was one way to dispel that alienation.

This theory was partly based on Richard Cloward and Lloyd Ohlim's work with juvenile delinquents. As a result the drafters of the poverty bill included a key provision—that the poverty program be "developed and conducted with the maximum feasible participation of the residents of the area."[82]

For many liberal reformers, participation of the poor in policy was not desirable. They had read the research on the political and social alienation of the poor and concluded that only the middle class exercised political rights of participation. Moynihan wrote in the late sixties in his diatribe, *Maximum Feasible Misunderstanding,* that the concept of participation was "social science...at its weakest, at its worst, when it offers theories...of bringing about mass behavioral change."[83]

Participation was the watchword of the 1960s. It was embodied in other guises by reformers. New Left radicals demanded "participatory democracy." Black Power militants called for black participation in the making of policy in those institutions affecting the lives of blacks. Community control advocates sought poor parents to be elected to urban school boards to make educational policy. These movements were not radical in nature but reformist, although they appeared extreme to many at that time. These reformers wanted to extend the democratic system to those it had bypassed—the poor.

Head Start was easily comprehensible; it was pre-school for the poor. Middle- and upper-class children had long enjoyed preschool. What made Head Start different was that not only was it for the children of the poor but it was based on startling evidence that children develop their mental capacities early. In his book, *Stability and Change in Human Characteristics,* Benjamin Bloom showed that children develop half their intelligence by the age of four and the other half by the age of eight. Consequently, early school intervention promised to reach the children of the poor at a crucial period.

Head Start was also to revolutionize preschool education. Preschool for middle-class children in America mostly meant socialization rather than emphasis on academics. However, Head Start, like the Montessori system devised in the 1920s, stressed academics. In time, the typical American preschool shifted its focus from socialization to learning.

The other part of Kennedy's unfulfilled agenda was federal aid to education, an issue that Johnson readily understood and championed.

Kennedy was unsuccessful in pressing Congress for federal aid to education. In addition to weak relations with Congress, he faced strong opposition among lobbying blocs. First, southern members of Congress were anxious over the possibility of school integration. Second, the Catholic church opposed any aid to public schools that would not also help Catholic schools.

By Johnson's ascendancy, some megaforces had changed. The civil rights movement was in full flower, pressuring Southern congressmen, and the reforms at Vatican Council softened the Catholic approach and opened up the possibility of compromise.

In the last analysis, however, Johnson's adroitness made the difference.

Basking in a national mandate with a landslide vote, he made the most of a prolonged "presidential honeymoon." For his part he was an able persuader.

Johnson's involvement in the educational policy process was twofold. First, he set broad policy. A close examination of the presidential policy process in the Higher Education Act (HEA) revealed his strong influence. Jose Chavez observed in his study that Johnson was mainly involved in setting broad policy and in influencing congressional legislators. Johnson established "the basic outline of the HEA proposal."[84] However, he was "not involved in the details of how the ideas were developed into programs."[85] That task belonged to his aides.

Second, he personally applied pressure on members of Congress. Johnson as a former Senate majority leader was a member of the club in Congress. He enjoyed the company of congressmen, intimately knew their ways and spent much time with them. Wilbur Cohen, a former Kennedy aide before becoming Johnson's secretary of Health, Welfare and Education, contrasted the styles of the two men. "Kennedy was never part of the 'inner circle' or the 'club' when he was in Congress," Cohen recalled.[86] "Congressmen looked upon Kennedy as 'a nice boy, but not as a guy who could get what he wanted.'[87] On the other hand, Johnson always acted like he was still on the inside looking out," Cohen contended.[88]

Then there was the "treatment." When Johnson wanted to have a certain bill passed, he would employ any stratagem. The treatment could involve tears, humor, mimicry or a combination. Hubert Humphrey observed that Johnson "was a master of working over people; not only working with people, but working them over."[89]

The treatment could bring a soft approach: an invitation to the targeted member of Congress to go "over to the White House for Lady Bird and myself to sit down with him and have lunch with him."[90] As a last resort, Johnson contacted the member's friends and family. He declared that "if I've got to call out somebody back home that's his friend to get him moving, I'll do it."[91] More drastic still was his calling up congressional wives to tell them that "your husband is not helping me."[92]

Johnson was well served by his first commissioner of education, Francis Keppel, whom he inherited from Kennedy. Keppel's main task was to negotiate with the special interests—the Catholic church, the National Education Association, Southern members of Congress. He performed ably.

A major reason for the success of Johnson and his aides was the type of federal aid that was proposed. Abandoning the general aid approach, they struck on the strategy of categorical aid, that is, aid targeted only for a specific national purpose, in this case, aid to the children of the poor. The idea was Wilbur Cohen's, another Kennedy aide; however, Keppel recalled that the bill "was largely put together in the first part of Mr. Johnson's time."[93]

Keppel credited six men with playing crucial roles that resulted in the passage of a federal aid to education bill. These were Presidents Kennedy and Johnson, conservative senators Robert Taft and Barry Goldwater, Pope John and Nikita Khrushchev. Johnson and Kennedy "just kept the pressure on"; Robert Taft set the stage with a "change of mind"; Barry Goldwater and his ill-timed conservatism gave the Democrats a landslide victory in 1964 "by increasing the Democrats in the house by a factor of seventy"; Pope John's *aggiornamento* created a climate in American Catholicism that encouraged "a willingness to negotiate"; and finally, Khrushchev "had managed in the late '50's through the Sputnik business to make people think that education was really important."[94]

The result was the Elementary and Secondary Education Act (ESEA) of 1965. The essence of ESEA was Title I, which was categorical aid to the children of the poor. The total outlay was an unprecedented $1 billion, which was minuscule by comparison to the national education cost. The cost of running New York City schools alone surpassed that amount. Since poverty was widespread, 95 percent of the counties in America qualified for aid. This fact prompted Senator Wayne Morse, instrumental in the passage of ESEA, to remark disingenuously that ESEA was "in some ways a general aid bill."[95]

The other parts of ESEA did not address poverty. Monies were allocated for libraries, regional research centers and state departments of education. The latter was a concession to the South, whose state departments of education were not as extensive or as qualified as those in other parts of the country.

The Johnson administration rushed the federal aid to education bill through Congress in less than three months. The bill passed the House on March 29, 1965, by a vote of 263 to 153; it passed the Senate on April 9 by a vote of 73 to 18. In a largely Democratic Congress, 98 percent of Northern Democrats in the House and 100 percent in the Senate supported the bill. On the other hand, only 27 percent of Southern Democrats in the House and 75 percent in the Senate voted for the bill, a vote indicating that racial issues die hard. On the whole, few of the Republican minority voted for the bill.[96]

Democrats were attuned to the poverty issue. Senator Wayne Morse (D-Ore.), who steered the bill through the Senate, concluded that "the impact of poverty in its various forms is a matter of national concern."[97] Indeed, Morse claimed that "even the limited opposition" to ESEA "has not denied the need for special progress and support for educationally deprived children."[98] Consequently, Morse argued that it is "only by such extra effort" as federal aid that "these children can be placed on an equal basis with other children."[99]

There were the predictable hurdles. Senator Ellender (D-La.) raised the constitutional issue; he pointed out that "there is no specific authority in the Constitution" for federal involvement in education.[100] Moreover, he was concerned over the church-state question so "that no money provided for in this bill will be paid directly to any school, other than public schools."[101]

There was the issue of federal control. Senator Prouty (R-V.) first raised that question. He distilled the debate over ESEA into "which is most important—the unmet needs of our schools and schoolchildren or the danger of insidious Federal involvement and control of the educational process?"[102]

Johnson was elated over the passage of ESEA. The Senate completed passage of the bill on a Friday, and Johnson quickly returned to his Texas ranch for a planned celebratory signing. In a highly symbolic gesture, Johnson signed ESEA on Sunday, April 11, at Junction School—the first school he attended from age four to grade eight. He orchestrated the event with eleven teachers from his schoolteaching years, nearly fifty of his former pupils and some of his classmates.[103] The education president wanted the proper setting for what he considered "the most significant education bill in the history of Congress."[104]

In sum, ESEA was a master stroke. It obviated long-standing opposition by employing categorical aid. Moreover, it continued a tradition in American education of a federal response to a national need. Lincoln signed the Morrill Land Grant Act to shore up a sagging agricultural economy; Roosevelt installed the G.I. Bill of Rights for veterans of World War II at a time when technology was on the rise; Eisenhower pushed for the National Defense Education Act as a response to Sputnik and Johnson provided federal aid to address the issue of poverty in America.

The Elementary and Secondary Education Act was quickly followed by the Higher Education Act of 1965, which further extended aid to the poor. Students were provided assistance in three ways: low interest loans, work-study programs and a scholarship program.

There were other educational breakthroughs in the Great Society. Bilingual programs were created with federal support, vocational educational programs were strengthened and the U.S. Office of Education was greatly expanded.

Lastly, the Great Society had a profound impact on the development of research, especially educational research. For the first time government programs were required to be evaluated. Concomitantly, large amounts of federal dollars were spent on research.

Educational research benefitted. Previously, educational research was rather uncomplicated: descriptive surveys of the status quo. With the Great Society educational research become more sophisticated. Experimental studies proliferated, and qualitative research, necessary in classroom settings, emerged. Policy studies were introduced, and evaluation became a popular tool for policy makers. Two observers of the Great Society programs commented that "before the 1960s there was very little interest in, and very little basis for, assessing the impact of governmental activities."[105] But "new techniques of evaluation," such as cost-benefit analysis and planning-program-budgeting-systems (PPBS), were begun so that "for the first time . . . programs and policies have been tested on the basis of performance."[106]

The equity school reform movement of the 1960s was fueled in large measure by Great Society educational programs. Johnson's able second commissioner of education, Harold Howe II, characterized the Great Society as part of the large-scale education reform movement. He argued:

> Most of the new money that would flow from the entitlement that Frank Keppel helped to get through the Congress for elementary and secondary schools was "*change*" money. That is, it was money aimed at helping the States and local school districts bring about new levels of activity, *changes* in programs, different kinds of services. . . . The objectives were institutional *change*, curricular *change*, organizational *change*, with an idea to helping the elementary and secondary schools meet the problems of modern America[107] (emphasis added).

Howe was candid on the role of the federal government in this change-agent capacity. He elaborated:

> The Federal Government . . . has taken the position [in devising these new legislative programs and administering them] that there are certain *national priorities* in education, that these can be identified; and that it's the business of the Administration and the Congress to figure out the most important directions for *change* in education and then to provide Federal money which will bring the *national priorities* and the direction for *change* together and allow the *change* to come about in terms of *national priorities*[108] (emphasis added).

CONCLUSION

How successful was the Great Society? On balance Great Society programs were reasonably effective, especially in education.

Conservative and neoconservative policy analysts claimed otherwise; for them the Great Society had failed. They maintained that the Great Society futilely spent large sums of money on social problems that would prove insoluble. Their crucial assumption—never proved—was that poverty was of one's own making. Political scientists such as Edward Banfield charged that poverty was the result of the inability to plan for the future.[109] Sociologists such as Nathan Glazer took that argument one step further by claiming that government was unable to respond to major social problems.[110] None of these conservative and neoconservative analysts took seriously substantive racial and sex discrimination in American life. They posited a nihilistic view of social policy that contrasted sharply with the liberal optimism of people like Michael Harrington.

Other assessments based on cumulative data challenged the nihilism of conservative analysts. Sar A. Levitan and Robert Taggart reviewed the literature of evaluative studies of Great Society programs in the mid-seventies. Their analysis, published under the title, *The Promise of Greatness,* established that the Great Society, far from being wastefully ineffective, was reasonably successful in achieving its goals.

Levitan and Taggart made a number of assessments of Great Society programs. Reviewing the studies of these programs, they concluded that the goals of the Great Society were realistic; that the social and racial programs "moved the nation toward a more just and equitable society";[111] that the welfare programs were reasonably efficient; and that as a result of the Great Society, America had reached a plateau in social policy.

In racial matters, Levitan and Taggart pointed to the 1965 Civil Rights Act and the 1965 Voting Rights Act. In health, there were Medicare and Medicaid. Manpower and job training programs achieved a certain measure of success. In education, programs had some notable impact.

Perhaps the largest success in education was the Head Start progam. It had been hastily dismissed early in its development; however, subsequent long-term (longitudinal) studies overwhelmingly indicated that Head Start was a brilliant stroke.

In the late sixties, an early evaluation by the Westinghouse Learning Corporation and Ohio State University charged that Head Start was largely a failure. The study's main thrust was that IQ gains purportedly attributed to children in Head Start disappeared by the first few years of regular school. President Nixon then branded the four-year-old program as "experimental" and "extremely weak."[112]

The Westinghouse study lingered in the minds of some conservative analysts long after the data proved erroneous. Indeed, as late as 1983, neo-conservative educational historian Diane Ravitch wrote that "the national evaluations repeatedly showed that the academic efforts of Head Start were limited and transitory."[113]

Long-term studies proved otherwise. In the late 1970s, Irving Lazar and Richard B. Darlington reviewed the host of Head Start studies from inception through the period 1976-1977. These studies consistently indicated academic gains. Head Start children were less likely to be retained in grade. On the whole, IQ gains lasted a full three years and in three projects were permanent. Fourth-grade Head Start children performed better on math and reading tests than their counterparts. Moreover, Head Start students indicated higher levels of self-esteem than did their counterparts. Lazar and Darlington concluded that "pre-school intervention programs had significant long-term effects on school performance."[114]

The key study that received widespread publicity was the Ypsilanti study. Editorialists and politicians cited this study in defense of Head Start. Moreover, a cost-conscious President Bush accepted its findings and pressed for an increase in Head Start funding.

The Ypsilanti study was a twenty-year longitudinal analysis of a Head Start project in Ypsilanti, Michigan. Published in 1984, it was entitled *Changed Lives: The Effect of the Perry Preschool Program on Youth Through Age 19*. The study presented long-term evidence in support of significant positive effects of Head Start on academic performance, citizenship, self-esteem and occupation.

The study involved a true experiment with randomization of subjects and a control group that was exposed to Head Start. The subjects numbered 123, all black and poor. The strength of longitudinal studies is an in-depth assessment over a prolonged period. However, this assessment necessitates a small sample, which constitutes a limitation of longitudinal research. The Ypsilanti study found that the Head Start youngsters excelled over their counterparts in every measure. Head Start students either attended college or held gainful employment to a degree double that of students in the control group. Head Start students were half as likely to become pregnant in their teenage years as were non–Head Start students. The high school dropout rate for Head Starters was reduced by 20 percent. Most importantly, the Head Starters performed better academically than their counterparts.

The authors of the Yspilanti study offered a cost-benefit implication to their research. They estimated the economic benefits that could be accrued by a Head Start student to be "over seven times the cost of one year of the program."[115] They concluded that "the evidence generated by longitudinal research on the effectiveness of early childhood education programs of high quality strongly supports decisions by policymakers to use public funds to expand such programs."[116]

How did Title I of ESEA, dealing with the poor, fare? First, the requirement for evaluation of Title I programs permitted wide discretion to the states and localities in evaluating their projects. Consequently, there was no uniform standard by which to compare the 20,000 initial projects.[117]

Still, by the early 1970s Title I projects did not show much success in educating the poor. A small study by the Department of Health, Education and Welfare in 1970 indicated poor results. This study reviewed 314 projects that employed the same reading test.[118] Another study completed by the Rand Corporation in the mid-seventies corroborated that earlier view. The Rand study reviewed projects from 1965 to 1972.[119]

By the early 1980s, Title I programs seemed to be making incremental gains. A study by the National Assessment for Progress indicated that poor, nine-year-old black students had raised their reading scores by 9.9 percent when compared to their counterparts in 1970-1971, 1974-1975 and 1979-1980. This incremental gain was attributed to the impact of Title I programs.[120]

There were other impacts of Title I. Samuel Halperin, the education aide in the Johnson administration largely responsible for writing ESEA, responded to critics by listing more intangible goals. He argued that ESEA "broke the logjam of federal aid to education"—certainly important in itself.[121] Moreover, he pointed out that ESEA "drastically changed the terms of congressional, and later, educational debate" by shifting the focus from teachers and their salary needs to the "special needs of children."[122] Finally, Halperin observed that a large impact was that ESEA "strengthens the federal system in education."[123]

In summary, the Great Society transformed education in America. Education became a major national issue that was addressed by a president of the United States who shaped an educational agenda. The Great Society defined the way issues of equity—poverty and civil rights—would be handled; the federal government projected that national agenda onto the states and localities. Not until the excellence reform movement of the 1980s would the federal government delegate that influence to the states.

Moreover, that federal influence was felt despite minimal funding by the government. Federal expenditures accounted for approximately 8 percent of the nation's education bill. Indeed, Samuel Halperin calculated that Title I monies never reached beyond a minuscule $200 per pupil per year for the 5 to 6 million poor students that Title I helped during the period 1965-1975—a low 3 percent increment in the cost of educating a poor student.[124] The expenses of a war in Vietnam did much to curtail government spending on Great Society programs.

In conclusion, Johnson became the education president against whom all others will be measured. He mounted a bully pulpit for the cause of public education and enacted far-reaching, innovative and substantive programs that have left their mark on America.

NOTES

1. Charles Dean McCoy, *The Education President: Lyndon Baines Johnson's Public Statements on Instruction and the Teaching Profession* (Austin: University of Texas Press, 1975), p. 74.

2. Ibid., p. 1.

3. Lyndon B. Johnson, *The Vantage Point: Perspective on the Presidency (1963-1969)* (New York: Holt, Rinehart and Winston, 1971), p. 19.

4. Lyndon B. Johnson, "The Goals: Ann Arbor," in *The Great Society Reader: The Failure of American Liberalism*, ed. Marvin E. Gettleman and David Mermelstein (New York: Random House, 1967), p. 15.

5. Francis Keppel, "Oral History Interview" (transcript), Austin, Tex., Lyndon B. Johnson Presidential Library, April 21, 1969, p. 7.

6. Wilbur Cohen, "Oral History Intreview" (transcript), Austin, Tex., Lyndon B. Johnson Presidential Library, March 2, 1969, tape 3, page 16.

7. Ibid.

8. George Reedy, *Lyndon B. Johnson: A Memoir* (New York: Andrews and McNeel, 1982), p. 22.

9. Keppel, "Oral History Interview," pp. 3-4.

10. Ibid.

11. Ibid., p. 11.

12. Douglass Cater, "Oral History Interview" (transcript), Austin, Tex., Lyndon B. Johnson Presidential Library, April 29, 1969, tape 1, p. 129.

13. Paul Charles Light, *President's Agenda: Domestic Policy Choice from Kennedy to Carter* (Baltimore: Johns Hopkins University Press, 1982), p. 70.

14. Arthur M. Schlesinger, Jr., *A Thousand Days: John F. Kennedy and the White House* (Boston: Houghton Mifflin, 1965), p. 849.

15. Frances Fox Piven and Richard A. Cloward, *Poor People's Movements: Why They Succeed, How They Fail* (New York: Random House, 1977), p. 189.

16. Aldon D. Morris, *The Origins of the Civil Rights Movement: Black Communities Organizing for Change* (New York: Free Press, 1984), p. 5.

17. Doris Kearns, *Lyndon Johnson and the American Dream* (New York: Harper and Row, 1976), p. 232.

18. Ibid.

19. David J. Garrow, *Bearing the Cross: Martin Luther King, Jr., and the Southern Christian Leadership Conference* (New York: Morrow, 1986), p. 548.

20. Ibid.

21. Piven and Cloward, *Poor People's Movements,* p. 246.

22. Kearns, *Lyndon Johnson and the American Dream,* p. 230.

23. Lyndon B. Johnson, "To Fulfill These Rights," in Gettleman and Mermelstein, *Great Society Reader,* p. 254.

24. Ibid., p. 258.

25. Ibid., p. 259.

26. Ibid.

27. Dwight MacDonald, "Our Invisible Poor," *New Yorker,* January 19, 1963, p. 82.

28. Michael Harrington, *The Other America: Poverty in the United States* (New York: Macmillan, 1962), p. 179.

29. Ibid., p. 2.

30. MacDonald, "Our Invisible Poor," p. 82.

31. *Book Review Digest* (New York: R.R. Bowker, 1963), p. 516.

32. Ibid.

33. Ibid.

34. Michael Harrington, *The Long-Distance Runner* (New York: Henry Holt, 1988), p. 224.

35. *New York Times,* October 7, 1987, p. B8.

36. Ibid.

37. Harrington, *The Other America,* p. 174.

38. Michael Harrington, *The New American Poverty* (New York: Holt, Rinehart and Winston, 1984), pp. 1-2.

39. Charles Murray, *Losing Ground: American Social Policy 1950-1980* (New York: Basic Books, 1984), p. 7.

40. Ibid., p. 8.

41. Ibid., p. 58.

42. Lyndon B. Johnson, *The Vantage Point,* p. 206.

43. Ibid., p. 207.

44. Ibid.

45. McCoy, *The Education President,* p. 82.

46. Ibid., p. 83.

47. Ibid.

48. Ibid.

49. Lyndon B. Johnson," State of the Union Message," *New York Times,* January 9, 1964, p. 16.

50. Ibid.

51. Cater, "Oral History," tape 1, p. 11.

52. Ibid.

53. Lyndon B. Johnson, "Acceptance Speech—Democratic Party National Convention," *New York Times,* August 28, 1964, p. 12.

54. Lyndon B. Johnson, "Inaugural Address," *New York Times,* January 21, 1965, p..16.

55. Lyndon B. Johnson, "Education Message," *New York Times,* January 13, 1965, p. 20.

56. Ibid., p. 24.

57. Ibid.

58. Lyndon B. Johnson, "State of the Union Message," *New York Times,* January 18, 1966, p. 14.

59. Ibid.

60. Lyndon B. Johnson, "State of the Union Message," *New York Times,* January 11, 1967, p. 16.

61. Ibid.

62. Lyndon B. Johnson, "State of the Union Message," *New York Times,* January 18, 1968, p. 16.

63. Cater, "Oral History," tape 2, p. 26.

64. Reedy, *Lyndon B. Johnson,* p. 77.

65. Ibid.

66. Ibid.

67. Eric F. Goldman, *The Tragedy of Lyndon Johnson* (New York: Knopf, 1969), p. 427.

68. Ibid., p. 430.

69. Kearns, *Lyndon Johnson and the American Dream,* p. 22.

70. Reedy, *Lyndon B. Johnson,* p. 34.

71. Ibid.

72. Ibid.

73. Robert Caro, *The Path To Power: The Early Years of Lyndon Johnson* (New York: Knopf, 1982), p. 129.

74. Ibid., p. 169.

75. Ibid., p. 206.

76. Julie Roy Jeffrey, *Education for the Children of the Poor* (Columbus: Ohio State University Press, 1978), p. 33.

77. Daniel Patrick Moynihan, *Maximum Feasible Misunderstanding* (New York: Free Press, 1969), p. xv.

78. Nelson F. Ashline et al., *Education, Inequality and National Policy* (Lexington, Mass.: Lexington Books, 1976), p. xvii.

79. Reedy, *Lyndon B. Johnson,* p. 22.

80. Ibid., p. 23.

81. Ibid., p. 13.

82. Moynihan, *Maximum Feasible Misunderstanding,* p. xvi.

83. Ibid., p. 191.

84. Jose Chavez, "Presidential Influence on the Politics of Higher Education: The Higher Education Act of 1965" (Ann Arbor, Mich.: University Microfibus, 1975), p. 107.

85. Ibid., pp. 107-10.

86. Cohen, "Oral History," tape 3, p. 24.

87. Ibid., p. 25.

88. Ibid.

89. McCoy, *Education President,* p. 147.

90. Ibid.

91. Ibid.

92. Ibid.

93. Keppel, "Oral History," p. 7.

94. Ibid., p. 17.

95. Jeffrey, *Education for the Children of the Poor,* p. 89.

96. Ibid., pp. 88-89.

97. *Congressional Record,* 89th Congress, 1st session, 1965 (Washington, D.C.: U.S. Government Printing Office), p. 7297.

98. Ibid.

99. Ibid.

100. Ibid., p. 7308.

101. Ibid.

102. Ibid., p. 7320.

103. *Daily Diary of President Lyndon B. Johnson* (Frederick, Md.: University Publications of America, 1980), pp. 3, 5.

104. Jeffrey, *Education for the Children of the Poor,* p. 98.

105. Sar A. Levitan and Robert Taggart, *The Promise of Greatness* (Cambridge, Mass.: Harvard University Press, 1976), pp. 4-5.

106. Ibid., p. 5.

107. Harold Howe II, "Oral History Interview" (transcript) Austin, Tex., Lyndon B. Johnson Presidential Library, July 12, 1968, p. 8.

108. Ibid., p. 16.

109. Edward Banfield, *The Unheavenly City* (Boston: Little, Brown, 1970).

110. Nathan Glazer, "The Limits of Social Policy," *Commentary,* September 1971.

111. Levitan and Taggart, *Promise of Greatness,* p. 8.

112. Maurice R. Berube, "Head Start to Nowhere, *Commonweal,* May 30, 1969, p. 311.

113. Diane Ravitch, *The Troubled Crusade: American Education 1945-1980* (New York: Basic Books, 1983), p. 159.

114. Irving Lazar and Richard B. Darlington, *Lasting Effects After Preschool* (Ithaca, N.Y.: Cornell University Press, 1978), p. 134.

115. David P. Weikart et al., *Changed Lives: The Effects of the Perry Preschool Program on Youths Through Age 19* (Ypsilanti, Mich.: High Scope Press, 1984), p. 1.

116. Ibid., p. xiii.

117. Jeffrey, *Education for the Children of the Poor*, p. 160.

118. Ibid., pp. 162-63.

119. Hugh Davis Graham, *The Uncertain Triumph: Federal Education Policy in the Kennedy and Johnson Years* (Chapel Hill: University of North Carolina Press, 1984), p. 207.

120. *New York Times*, April 29, 1981, p. A20.

121. Samuel Halperin, "ESEA: The Positive Side," *Phi Delta Kappan*, November 1975, p. 147.

122. Ibid., p. 118.

123. Ibid., p. 150.

124. Ibid., p. 147.

5

Ronald Reagan (1981–1989) and the Excellence Reform Movement

Ironically, the second education president of modern times was Ronald Reagan. Reagan became an education president by accident. He did not intend either to reform or to strongly influence education in this country; indeed, he favored shoring up private schooling and decreasing federal funds and the federal role in public education. In 1980, he made a campaign pledge to dismantle the newly created Department of Education.

How did Ronald Reagan, then, become an education president? Simply, Reagan responded to the major outside societal force of his era: foreign economic competition. With the publication of the Department of Education's jeremiad, *A Nation at Risk: The Imperative for Education Reform,* the excellence reform movement was officially launched. The aim of the excellence reform movement was to raise educational standards to groom the best and the brightest students so as to make America once again economically competitive. Education reform became a national political issue, and Ronald Reagan recognized a good idea when he saw it. Through the use of a bully pulpit, he preached the virtues of excellence reform.

The national direction in education reform provided by President Reagan was largely symbolic. He was the chief cheerleader to focus the nation's attention on school reform. He initiated no new federal education programs and constantly sought to reduce the federal budget in education. In education, his was a rhetorical presidency.

THE ECONOMY

By the 1980s, the American public and its national leaders once again perceived the link between economic well-being and American education.

The clear economic dominance of Japan laid the foundation for alarm in the American psyche. The underlying assumption of the education reformers of the 1980s was that economic recovery depended on the revitalization of American education. Presidents could no longer relegate education to the bottom drawer of presidential priorities.

A number of scholarly studies were published detailing America's continuing economic decline in the 1980s. Their themes were similar. American business had lost the competitive race because of shortsightedness and greed. Through its policies American government had supported the short-term profits at the expense of long-term gains. Most importantly, a combination of an enormous federal deficit and bloated military spending had made the United States a debtor nation.

Two such studies received widespread hearing. One was from a Yale historian, and the other was from a Harvard economist. The historian presented a long-range perspective, and the economist reviewed recent policies. Each complemented the other.

Paul Kennedy, professor of history at Yale, presented an overview since the Renaissance. His thesis was simple but nonetheless powerful: the great nations first prospered economically, than expanded militarily over a global network to protect their new markets until military overexpansion drained the economic reserves of the national government. His book was entitled *The Rise and Fall of the Great Powers: Economic Change and Military Conflict from 1500 to 2000*. It documented the process in Spain, France and England in the past and currently for the United States and the Soviet Union.

Kennedy argued that the United States was guilty of "imperial overstretch."[1] First, the economy began to decline under global competition. The United States accounted for a smaller share of the world's manufacturing market. American agriculture had also declined as a share of the world's market. The result was a trade deficit. Compounding this process was an enormous military obligation to preserve global arrangements made at the height of American economic power. "The United States today has roughly the same massive array of military obligations across the globe as it had a quarter century ago," Kennedy observed, "when its share of the GNP ... was so much larger than it is now."[2]

The question for Kennedy was whether the United States "can preserve a reasonable balance between the nation's perceived defense requirements ... and ... [the] economic bases of its power" in the face of global economic competition.[3]

Benjamin M. Friedman, a Harvard University economist, reinforced the decline thesis from another perspective. His was a microanalysis in contrast to Kennedy's macroanalysis. Friedman accused the Reagan administration in the 1980s of embarking on a "radical course" by "pursuing a policy that amounts to living not just in, but for, the present."[4] According to Friedman,

Reagan policy was based on three disastrous ideas: high military spending, business tax cuts and industry deregulation. Consequently, America no longer was a producing country, but a consuming one, which would sell off its prize assets to pay for consumption. As a result, the United States became a debtor nation for the first time in the modern age, with an enormous federal budget deficit and national trade deficit.

Friedman documented the large budget deficits of the Reagan years. When Reagan came into office in 1980, he assumed a $79 billion budget deficit from Jimmy Carter, with a total national debt of $914 billion. In the next six years, the Reagan budget deficits dwarfed those of his predecessor. Increased military spending largely accounted for an average $184 billion budget deficit in each of those six years. By 1987, the budget deficit, anchored on the largest military buildup in peacetime, totaled $2.6 trillion dollars.[5]

A trade deficit followed. By 1987, foreign imports exceeded American imports by $159 billion. America was a full-fledged debtor nation—a position to which she was not accustomed. Still, according to Friedman, there was a cultural lag in realizing this new arrangement. "Most Americans," Friedman contended, "continue to think of themselves as creditors."[6] However, Friedman foresaw dim prospects. "Economically stagnant countries cannot lead the world," he wrote, "no matter what their military strength."[7]

Most importantly, American businesses had not used tax cuts to invest and refurbish their industries. There was a smaller rate of investment to create new wealth; rather, there was a decline. In the three decades prior to the 1980s, American investment averaged 3.3 percent of total income.[8] During the Reagan years, the average dropped to 2.3 percent of total income.[9] Part of that drop was the consequence of new tax and regulatory policies that permitted corporations to use extra funds to buy out other companies rather than reinvest. In many cases, those companies were sold, in turn, to foreign investors to make a quick profit.[10]

"We are selling off America," Friedman warned, "and living off the proceeds." Friedman observed that "we are not borrowing against the future earning power of our new industries, for there are none."[11] Instead, he argued, "we are simply mortgaging our future living standard."[12] Yet our competitors, such as France, West Germany and Japan, are essentially demilitarized nations that rely on America for their defense.

Still, neither Kennedy nor Friedman was a Cassandra. They both believed that the process could be reversed with enlightened government and American business practices.

REAGAN'S EDUCATIONAL PHILOSOPHY

Ronald Reagan cannot be said to have had a coherent educational philosophy. His educational ideas were more often a gut reaction to liberal's espousal of education and the federal role. Perhaps his strongest feelings as he came into the White House involved the restoration of school prayer in the public schools through a constitutional amendment. Along with many conservatives, Reagan perceived school prayer to be the cornerstone in restoring discipline, respect and motivation in the classrooms of America.

Concomitantly, Reagan abhorred the growing federal role in education. Although the federal government did not have a substantially financial function in paying for American education (never totaling more than 10 percent of the national education bill), the influence of the federal government had been paramount in setting the national education agenda since Lyndon Johnson. Reagan believed that the states should be the primary educational agent. Consequently, he initially wanted to eliminate the newly created Department of Education and substantially cut federal aid to education.

On the other hand, President Reagan believed in shoring up private education. He was convinced that such strategies as a voucher system and tuition tax credits would enable students to have a choice in education and provide private schools with a much needed infusion of public monies. The voucher system involves the federal government's issuing monies to students to pay for their education at the school of their choice—public, private or parochial. The Reagan administration introduced such a plan involving poor children under Chapter I. Tuition tax credits would permit parents with children in private or parochial schools to deduct the cost of their children's education on their income taxes. Both proposals were successfully opposed by the teacher unions, which were concerned about the erosion of public education.

Reagan sought to reduce federal aid to education substantially during his tenure. Reagan's budgets projected huge cuts in education spending, at times amounting to one-third below previous spending. Only his 1985 budget—after the publication of *A Nation at Risk* and an election year—reflected a slight increase. Democrats in Congress withstood many of the proposed cuts. However, the net result was that Department of Education budgets declined from 2.5 percent of the national budget to 1.8 percent during the Reagan years.[13]

In 1981, Reagan requested an education budget of $13.5 billion, 6 percent less than the previous year; Congress increased the sum to $14.8 billion.[14] In 1982, Reagan requested a $12.4 billion education budget, 16 percent less than was finally appropriated: $14.8 billion, the same as had been finally appropriated in 1981.[15]

In 1983, the Reagan request was for $9.95 billion, less than that appropriated the previous year; Congress raised that to $15.4 billion. In 1984, Reagan asked for more money than he had the previous year, $13.2 billion, but this request was at least 14.5 percent less than was appropriated by Congress the previous year. In 1985, in the budget request for the election year ($15.48 billion), he asked for slightly above what Congress appropriated, a sharp increase from previous administration requests; Congress, in response to the excellence reform movement, approved a budget of $19.1 billion, then an all-time high. In 1986, Reagan reduced his request sharply to $15.5 billion, 18 percent less than what Congress had appropriated the previous year; Congress cut back from the previous year's allocation to $17.9 billion, but almost $2.5 billion more than the president had wanted. In 1987, Reagan asked for $15.2 billion, 15 percent less than Congress had enacted the previous year; Congress increased spending on education once again to $19.7 billion. In 1988, Reagan's last year, the administration requested $14 billion, 29 percent lower than Congress had voted the previous year; Congress responded by reaching a $20.3 billion education budget.[16]

Most importantly, the cuts in federal aid were aimed at programs that the administration did not favor. Bilingual programs were cut 54 percent during the Reagan years.[17] Compensatory education programs for the poor declined by 25 percent.[18]

On the other hand, Reagan proposed spending programs that would invigorate private education. In 1983, he proposed a $300 tax deduction to families who paid tuition in private and parochial schools.[19] He offered poor students under Chapter I a $600 voucher for the same purpose. Neither proposal was politically feasible at the time.

REAGAN'S EARLY INFLUENCES

Three major influences seem to have influenced Ronald Reagan early in life. The first was negative and, perhaps, the most powerful. The young Ronald had to contend with his father's alcoholism. So strong an influence was this in young Ronald's life that he mentions it first in his ghostwritten autobiography before introducing his mother or other events in his life. He depicts the scene when he first encountered his father, Jack, drunk on the front porch in winter.[20] Ronald, eleven years old at that time, was forced to bring his father into the house. The memory lingered, as did his father's itinerant and marginal career as a shoe salesman, which resulted in the family's moving six times before Ronald went to college.

The second influence was more pleasant. His mother, Nelle, was for him the embodiment of sweetness "where no diploma was needed for kindness."[21] Moreover, Nelle Reagan had a cultural bent, giving "readings" for various ladies' societies."[22]

The third influence was educational. For Reagan, Eureka College was no less than "another home."[23] He found it to be "one of the loveliest colleges in existence" so that he "wanted to get in that school so badly that it hurt when I thought about it."[24]

Eureka, at the height of the depression, was a small Christian college with a student body of 250. Although poor, Reagan was able to attend through a tuition athletic scholarship for football and swimming and a job on campus to pay the board.

At Eureka, two events stood out. Reagan developed a love for the theater and acted in college productions, and in his freshman year, he exercised leadership potential. Reagan became the leader of a student strike that garnered national attention. Because of fiscal constraints the trustees had retrenched some courses that juniors and seniors needed for graduation. Young Reagan led his classmates in a boycott of classes in protest. The students won, and Ronald Reagan characterized his role as one of "polite resistance."[25]

In addition to the autobiography, Reagan has published only one other book, a collection of his speeches printed in 1968 when he was governor of California: *The Creative Society*. It gave a preliminary glimpse of his ideas, some of them educational, before he became a national political figure.

Two of the 21 addresses collected in *The Creative Society* involved higher education. In a speech on the Berkeley student revolt of 1964, Reagan, unfortunately, resorted to inflammatory rhetoric and questionable red-baiting. He characterized the student uprising as the result of "a leadership gap and a morality gap and a decency gap."[26] That rebellion, according to Reagan, had occurred because "the campus has become a rallying point for Communists and a center of sexual misconduct."[27] What encouraged such conduct, he contended, was a liberal professoriat that attempted to "indoctrinate."[28]

More importantly, he scored the lack of a core curriculum: "But so is the student wrong who would eliminate all required courses and grades— who would make education a kind of a four-year smorgasbord in which he would be the sole judge of how far and fast he ran in the pursuit of knowledge."[29]

Finally, in his criticism of academic liberalism he cited the underlying conservative ethos of social mobility. For Governor Reagan the fault for our success or lack of it lay not in the stars but in ourselves:

The student generation is being wooed by many who charge that this way we have known is inadequate to meet the challenge of our times. They point to the unsolved problems of poverty and prejudice as proof of the system's failure.

But students have a duty to find out if the failure is one of the system's—or is it the inadequacy of human nature?[30]

REAGAN AS GOVERNOR

There is nothing in Ronald Reagan's political past to indicate that he considered education a priority; however, he did display a capacity to compromise on education-spending bills while governor of California. He displayed this pragmatic sense again with the publication of *A Nation at Risk*. In the eight years that Reagan was governor of California (1967-1974), he emphasized issues other than education. Indeed, Reagan read almost wholly on foreign affairs; none of his close associates were from the educational establishment and, more importantly, some observers contend that his advisers did not prepare him sufficiently on educational issues.

Reagan's only educational interest was his desire to fire the president of the University of California, Clark Kerr. He viewed Kerr as the archetypical academic liberal whose inability to discipline the rebellious Berkeley students fueled a national college student uprising.

More typical of Reagan's views on education was his disdain for academic research, which he saw as a needless taxpayer expense to "subsidize intellectual curiosity."[31] What interest he did have in education was in private schooling. One educational journalist who covered his governorship observed that Reagan's "benign neglect of public higher education" was due to his own experience as a student at a private college.[32] Moreover, Reagan did not share "in the liberal vision of education as a tool with which to reform society."[33] His ideas were to strengthen private schools through tuition tax credits and vouchers. As early as 1970, Reagan declared that he was "interested in the educational voucher system for financing the education of our children."[34]

Nevertheless, his record on education when he was governor drew mixed reviews. He displayed a pragmatic sense in the face of an overwhelming Democratic legislature and a strong state Department of Education committed to education spending. Reagan education budgets substantially increased during his tenure, even when one allows for inflation; these increases muted criticism from traditional foes—the teacher unions. Indeed, the chief lobbyist for the California Teachers Association (affiliate of the National Education Association) concluded that "we didn't get everything we asked for, but overall his record for elementary and secondary education was good."[35] On the other hand, the lobbyist for California School Administrators characterized Reagan's record on school finance as good "but mostly unintentional."[36]

The reason for the acclaim was Reagan's active role in securing a compromise on a major school finance reform bill. Popularly called the Reagan-Moretti bill after the governor and the Democratic speaker of the assembly, this bill was a particular compromise over contending educational and political factions. Each interest group was able to secure some of its demands.

The Reagan-Moretti bill was a response to the movement of education finance reformers to make public school funding more equitable. The California Supreme Court in 1971 had ruled in the *Serrano* decision that education funding based on property taxes was unjust. The court mandated a new formula to fund schools that would not be based on the value of one's property, which varies from rich and poor areas, creating inequality of resources for education. The Reagan-Moretti bill was a classic political response to a classic American school problem.

Every interest group wanted a piece of the solution. Reagan desired property tax relief. The education lobby wanted more money spent on the schools. The education finance reformers sought an equitable equalization formula. The compromise satisfied Reagan and most of the education lobby. However, some education finance reformers considered the Reagan-Moretti bill a "fiscal Frankenstein."[37] Still, it showed that Ronald Reagan could be sufficiently flexible politically.

EXCELLENCE REFORM

The publication of the U.S. Department of Education's short study *A Nation at Risk: The Imperative for Educational Reform* triggered the excellence school reform movement in the 1980s. Published in April 1983, that report, in concert with other studies by educational and business groups, touched a public nerve. The short-term effect was to make education a presidential campaign issue in 1984. The report prodded Ronald Reagan into assuming a leadership role in education reform and earned him serious consideration as an education president.

It was the right issue at the right time. The American economy had been flagging. Foreign competition, especially the technological advances made by Japan, had made us a debtor nation, with foreign exports behind imports. Scholars were discussing the decline of the United States into a second-rate nation. A worried public implored their political representatives for drastic action. Initially, blame for the decline was placed on business. A small cottage industry of management books was published, almost wholly worshiping successful Japanese management techniques. In time, the focus shifted to the public schools, where America's brainpower to offset unfavorable economic competition resided.

A Nation at Risk was both an indictment of past educational sins and a hopeful solution to the nation's troubles. By 1984, educational reform was a campaign issue. Sensing the shifting political winds, President Reagan adopted educational reform. He reversed himself on the abolition of the Department of Education, and he muted his callls for prayer in the schools, tuition tax credits and vouchers. Most importantly, he used his office to maintain a steady drumbeat for educational reform and delivered many major speeches calling for educational reform. Through this use of the bully pulpit, he earned the right to be termed an education president.

It must be noted that excellence reform was a movement suited to the conservative philosophy of the president. The essence of excellence reform was to raise standards within the matrix of the current decentralized structure of public education in the United States. States were to assume the main burden of implementing reforms. The role of the federal government would be limited, and no new spending programs would be needed.

What was excellence reform and how did it come about? Essentially excellence reform meant raising student and teacher standards in the public schools. The Department of Education's report, *A Nation at Risk: The Imperative for School Reform,* set the excellence reform movement in motion. The widespread publicity and concomitant public interest made education a national issue.

A Nation at Risk was not the only report urging the upgrading of the American school system; a plethora of reports from foundations and business groups struck a similar note, but *A Nation at Risk* had the greatest impact. Secretary of Education Terrel Bell had hoped for an "attention getter" that would be "hard- hitting" and "critical."[38] His panel of outside educators delivered to him just that. Bell was delighted that the report would serve as "a warning as well as indictment to all of us—parents, educators, political leaders, taxpayers, and students."[39]

A Nation at Risk was deliberately alarmist. "If an unfriendly foreign power had attempted to impose on America the mediocre performance that exists today," the authors intoned in a now classic passage, "we might have viewed it as an act of war."[40] Five years later the education editor of the *New York Times,* Edward D. Fiske, characterized *A Nation at Risk* as deliberately "full of apocalyptic rhetoric and military analogies" to acomplish its goal of sounding an education alarm.[41] The report, he claimed, constituted "a blatantly political treatise, more legal brief than scholarly analysis."[42] Fiske claimed that in order to maintain their argument, the authors of *A Nation at Risk* "pointedly ignored data that standardized tests scores had been on the rise for a number of years."[43]

The major charges of *A Nation at Risk* were fivefold. First, the report charged that American students compared unfavorably academically with foreign students for democratic countries. Second, the report showed that scores on the Scholastic Aptitude Tests (SATs) had declined for over a generation for college-bound seniors. Third, the report cited evidence indicating that high school seniors were weak in inferential skills. Fourth, the authors pointed out that student achievement in science had declined. Fifth, *A Nation at Risk* highlighted the national problem of illiteracy.

Critics charged that this "excellence" report was not so excellent in its argument. They claimed serious statistical misinterpretations. For example, some scholars charged that international comparisons were muddled, with an open American public school system being compared with selective foreign school systems. They added that studies indicated that the SAT decline was largely explained by a greater pool of college-bound seniors, many from lower socioeconomic background and concomitantly poorer academic preparation. This rising pool of applicants correlated with the success of the civil rights movement in opening up occupational doors. Finally, these critics maintained that the same national study that revealed lower inferential skills also indicated rising reading scores of younger students. However, other excellence studies were more sound in documenting the deficiencies of American public school students.[44]

A Nation at Risk recommended five main reforms. Of these, two involved considerable money. The report suggested lengthening the school day and the school year—a move that would significantly increase the number of teachers and the cost of public education—and the report called for the raising of teacher salaries, mainly through the mechanism of merit pay.

President Reagan's reading of *A Nation at Risk* left much to be desired. He perceived the report as cost-free education reform. For Reagan *A Nation at Risk* meant that "American schools don't need vast new sums of money as much as they need a few fundamental reforms."[45]

Indeed, *A Nation at Risk* was deliberately negligent on spelling out the dollar amounts. It was a policy without resources. According to Bell, the report deliberately "did not fix the level—federal, state or local—from which this funding should come."[46] Although Bell had no exact foreknowledge of what the authors of the report would say, there was agreement not "to embarrass the president."[47] The authors of the report solved this delicate problem by merely implying that the cost of reform should be assumed by the states.

Still, Reagan was in agreement with the general thrust of *A Nation at Risk*. He approved of the raising of academic standards for teachers and students and returning to a core curriculum to promote cultural literacy— major recommendations of *A Nation at Risk*. However, his distillation of *A Nation at Risk* shifted much of the focus to nonschool variables that elude policy controls—such as restoring discipline, ending drug and alcohol abuse and restoring parental influence.

Reagan's basic speech in favor of excellence reform included six steps emphasizing the aforementioned in addition to raising academic standards and returning educational leadership to state and local governments. The key issue for him and the excellence reformers was who was to blame for educational failure and who could remedy the situation. For the equity reformers of the sixties, the schools were to blame for student failure and the schools were entrusted with the obligation to do all in their power to educate youth. The crucial assumption of the equity reformers was that the schools could solve all the problems of society. President Lyndon Johnson typified this belief when he declared that education "was the answer for all our problems, the answer for all problems of the world."[48]

By contrast, the excellence reformers placed the focus on the student. These reformers felt that what the student brought to school was most important and that the job of the schools was to refine that native ability. Moreover, schools had been asked, as a result of the equity school reform movement, to do too much. They were being asked to solve all of the problems created by society in addition to teaching students academic subjects. Schools were perceived as the area to combat drugs, a possible AIDS epidemic, broken families, crime—in short, to solve the problems of society.

For neoconservative historian Diane Ravitch, this situation was simply a case of overburden. Exemplifying the rationale of the excellence reformers, she observed: "Throughout history, Americans have expected much of their educational institutions; sometimes schools have been expected to take on responsibilities for which they were entirely unsuited. When they have failed, it was because their leaders and public alike had forgotten their real limitations."[49]

Equity reformers retorted that few institutions outside the school were sufficiently equipped or interested to help alleviate many social problems. Consequently, the school was the social agency of last resort.

For President Reagan, the lesson was clear: the burden should be placed on parents not government. He limited the role of government in education: "Advocates of more and more government interference in education have had ample time to make their case and they've failed.[50]

He then charged parents that "education does not begin with Washington officials or even state and local officials" but that "it begins in the home where it is the right and responsibility of every American."[51] Consequently, Reagan admonished the educational system to "restore parents ... to their rightful place in the educational process."[52]

THE POLITICS OF A NATION AT RISK

If any man was single-handedly responsible for the excellence school reform movement, he was Terrel Bell. As Reagan's first secretary of education, Bell commissioned *A Nation at Risk* without presidential approval. He surreptitiously engineered a report he knew would be critical of education. His aim was to prod the president into exercising leadership in education. In the process he launched a school reform movement.

Bell was the only "outsider" in the Reagan cabinet. He was a typical representative of the educational establishment and was committed to public education and in favor of strong federal leadership. Recommending him to President Reagan were two stints as U.S. commissioner of education under Nixon and Ford; however, a moderate Republican, he was not in the same extreme, conservative ideological mold of Reagan advisers.

Bell's life history was a common Great Depression story. Terrel was eight when his father died, leaving his mother and nine children penniless. By a combination of pluck and federal largesse, he was able to obtain a college education and eventually rose to the top of the educational ladder. His mother set a strong example of self-help. She instructed the young Terrel to "present [myself] in a college registration line and see what happened. ... If I did that, things will work out some way or the other."[53]

Bell attended a teacher training institution, Albion State Normal School, because it was the cheapest. Tuition and fees were $11.50 per term. A part-time job with President Roosevelt's National Youth Administration (NYA) provided $17 a month—enough for college. He reflected later:

Without the NYA's $17 per month and Albion's $11.50 per term bargain-basement tuition, I would have missed the marvelous world of books, libraries, intellectual excitement, and all that learning which is beyond high school. This grubby little school with its inconsequential name had high standards, an atmosphere of creative tension, and a remarkably able faculty.[54]

His education was interrupted by World War II. He spent three and a half years in the Pacific as a marine. Later, he returned to college on the G.I. Bill of Rights. Bell never forgot the lesson of government aid to education.

His selection by Reagan appears to have been the product of a misunderstanding. Reagan was committed to abolishing the Department of Education; Bell was not. Furthermore, Bell recoiled from the hard-line conservatism of Reagan advisers, whom he described in his memoirs as "movement conservatives."

After being interviewed by Edward Meese, Reagan's chief adviser and, according to Bell, "the champion of the far right in the White House," Bell decided not to accept a cabinet post as secretary of education.[55] Meese had called the Department of Education "a great bureaucratic joke" and outlined a conservative agenda that would eventually eliminate federal aid to public education and furnish aid to private schooling.[56] Bell concluded after the interview that "the new Reagan administration was not for me."[57] However, he changed his mind after a subsequent interview with Reagan, as he believed Reagan to be more flexible than were his advisers. Bell was optimistic that he could convert the new president to the cause of public education.

This hope motivated Bell through his four-year tenure as "thirteenth" man in the Reagan cabinet. Bell compared his role to that of a "zealot," similar to the hard-line conservative ideologues, differing only in that he was "a missionary ready to preach the gospel of education to the Reaganites."[58] His main target was Reagan himself, whom he hoped to "persuade . . . to endorse what must be done for the learning society that America must become if it is to survive and achieve its destiny."[59]

In the end he felt he had failed. He concluded that in his term as secretary of education he "was not able to persuade President Reagan to see the connection between education and his first priority of building military power."[60] His estimate may have been clouded by his being a victim of office politics—an ideological outsider—who was not asked to continue into the second Reagan term.

Bell intended no less than to "stage an event that would jar the people into action on behalf of their educational system."[61] He wanted to commission a panel of prestigious—and like-minded—educators who would be "charged by the president himself to perform the task of appraising the conditions of our schools and reporting to the nation on what should be done."[62]

Unfortunately, he was rebuffed by the White House. Reagan aides informed him that reports of federal commissions usually had little impact and, more importantly, that education was the province of the states.

Undaunted, Bell proceeded to make a bold gamble. He commissioned the study within his own jurisdiction as secretary of education—without the imprimatur of the president's office. This action brought down on him the "movement conservatives" who considered his ploy tantamount to "an act of insubordination."[63] The gamble eventually cost him his job.

However, the report generated an educational revolution. *A Nation at Risk* caught Reagan by surprise. His first speech in support of the new study mainly rehashed his old educational agenda of school prayer and tuition tax credits, with minor mention of excellence issues, but as Reagan perceived the political windfall that Bell had wrought, his speeches grew stronger and more knowledgeable in support of excellence issues. In his first term he gave fifty-one major speeches "in which he had impressed the American people with the vital importance of education and the need for reform."[64] Bell had succeeded in converting Ronald Reagan to the cause of public education. For Bell, Reagan had become "a fantastic endorser of our efforts to build momentum for school reform."[65] Through use of the bully pulpit, Ronald Reagan could truly be said to have been largely responsible for the excellence school reform movement of the 1980s.

In turn, Ronald Reagan's newfound interest in education caught the American public off-guard. Hugh Sidey, columnist of *Time* magazine—a journal friendly to the Reagan administration—wondered about "Ronald Reagan's surprising concern over the education problems in the United States."[66] *Time* realized that, at bottom, Reagan's concern had a political element. *Time* writers described Reagan's newfound interest in education as a "course in politics" in which Reagan would "try for high marks in education."[67] They mused that adding education to the campaign issue list might mean that Ronald Reagan would once again attract women and blue-collar voters who had strayed from his 1980 coalition. *Time* quoted a White House aide who commented that "with education you reach out beyond liberal-conservative lines."[68]

Some critics felt that Reagan was merely a political opportunist exploiting the education issue. In time, Terrel Bell became one of those critics. After he was forced to resign in 1985, Bell concluded rather pessimistically that Reagan had not become an education president.

We could have changed the course of history in American education had the president stayed with us through the implementation phase of the school reform movement.

And this would have won a place in history for Ronald Reagan as the man who renewed and reformed education at a time when the nation was, indeed, at risk because we were not adequately educating our people to live effectively and competitively.[69]

There is some credence to that argument, but in the larger perspective, Ronald Reagan still emerges as an education president.

The evidence doesn't support Bell on two counts. First, Reagan did keep up a steady drumbeat for school reform in most State of the Union messages. Second, he appointed as Bell's successor William Bennett, who became the strongest education official since Harold Howe II had held the post in the Johnson administration. Bennett kept excellence reform as a major focus of Reagan's second term.

Reagan only passingly referred to education in his major public speeches before *A Nation at Risk* was issued. He failed to mention education in his inaugural speech and that same year mentioned education only in terms of proposed budget cuts. Neither did he mention education in his 1982 State of the Union message.

As the machinery for *A Nation at Risk* was being established, Reagan warmed to the task. In his 1983 State of the Union message—three months before *A Nation at Risk*—Reagan perceived the need to establish a superior educational system to compete with Japanese economic power. He told the American public:

We Americans are still the world's technological leader in most fields. We must keep the edge, and to do so we need to begin renewing the basics—starting with our educational system. While we grew complacent, others have acted. Japan, with a population only half the size of ours, graduates from its universities more engineers than we do. If a child does not receive adequate math and science teaching by the age of 16, he or she has lost the chance to be a scientist or engineer.

We must join together—parents, teachers, grassroots groups, organized labor and the business community—to revitalize American education by setting a standard of excellence.[70]

In an unusual extended section on education in this State of the Union-message, Reagan proposed four major education goals: (1) quality education, upgrading math and science; (2) education savings accounts for average Americans to save for college; (3) vouchers to permit children to attend "private or religiously affiliated schools"; and (4) a constitutional amendment to permit school prayer.[71] It is instructive that in this address, Reagan invoked America "to set a standard of *excellence*" (emphasis added). This was an early usage of the term that would characterize the school reform movement of the 1980s.

A year later, Reagan in his 1984 State of the Union message proudly proclaimed that he had established the National Commission on Excellence in Education that produced *A Nation at Risk*. He gloated that after a short year's time, "schools are reporting progress in math and reading skills" but that America must "encourage the teaching of basics" and "enforce tougher standards."[72]

His second inaugural address neglected the topic of education, as had the first. However, his 1985 State of the Union message presented another glowing report card on excellence reform. "We're returning to excellence," he informed the American people.[73] Schools were stressing "basics of discipline, rigorous testing and homework." He concluded, "We must go forward in our commitment to the new basics."[74]

He continued essentially the same message in his 1986 State of the Union message, albeit with the added ingredients of vouchers and school prayer. He spoke of "the renaissance in education" reflected in "the rising SAT scores for three years."[75] This was the work of "the American people, who, in reaching for excellence...turned education around."[76]

By 1987, Reagan's State of the Union message weakly addressed drugs contaminating the learning environment and no more, but in his last State of the Union message in 1988, he returned to excellence reform with a vengeance:

We all know the sorry story of the 60s and 70s—soaring spending, plummeting test scores—and that hopeful trend of the 80s, when we replaced an obsession with dollars with a commitment to quality, and test scores started back up. There is a lesson here that we should write on the blackboard a hundred times—in a child's education, money can never take the place of basics like discipline, hard work, and yes, homework....

How can we help? Well, we can talk about and push for these reforms. But the most important thing we can do is reaffirm that control of schools belongs to the states, local communities, and most of all, to the parents and teachers.[77]

In his last major address, a farewell at the Republican national convention in 1988, Reagan made only passing reference to education. He referred only to future needs of the nation in this regard: school prayer and the recitation of the Pledge of Allegiance.[78] The latter was to become a major campaign issue for George Bush, and one suspects that Reagan tailored his speech to aid his vice-president in the campaign ahead.

On balance, Reagan maintained a constant bully pulpit on education in his most august speeches, the State of the Union messages. Rather than forgetting education after the 1984 re-election campaign, as Bell charged, he became stronger in his commitment to excellence reform.

Reagan's radio talks during his first term evidenced his concern for education. Of 125 radio addresses, 35 were devoted to domestic social issues, and 10 discussed education. The first 2 radio talks in 1982 reiterated Reagan's initial favorite educational issues of tuition tax credits and returning prayer to public schools. Shortly before the publication of *A Nation at Risk* in March 1983, Reagan addressed the nation with a blend of old and new excellence issues. He admonished the United States to "strengthen its defenses, modernize its industries, and move confidently into a new era of high technology" by "restoring... excellence in our schools."[79] Again, the keyword "excellence" was sounded early; however, Reagan proposed solutions that were a familiar recipe: tuition tax credits, vouchers and prayer in the schools.

By the publication of *A Nation at Risk,* the radio talks on education sounded more assured. In April 1983, he reiterated for America the "disturbing report this week by the National Commission on Excellence in Education that I created."[80] He noted that *A Nation at Risk* "indicates the quality of learning in our classrooms has been declining for the last two decades."[81] He cited the study's recommendations for a core curriculum "requiring 4 years of English in high school and 3 solid years, each, of math and science."[82] Again, Reagan tacked on his pet notions of tuition tax credits and vouchers "to restore parental choice and influence and to increase competition between schools."[83]

A year later Reagan cheerfully informed the American people on the improved American educational report card. He declared that "we may have stemmed the rising tide of mediocrity with a tidal wave of school reforms."[84] He reviewed the increasing number of states that raised high school graduation requirements, made strong curriculum changes and commissioned educational task forces. He concluded that the "entire reform money is the only answer to the problems of our schools."[85] There was no mention of strategies such as tuition tax credits and vouchers to shore up private and parochial schooling.

In his last talk on education as schools reopened in September, Reagan took on the mantle of parent to the nation's schoolchildren. Although he stated that he didn't want to "sound like a scolding parent," he admonished students for "watching too much TV."[86] He had a bold objective—"to regain at least half of what he lost in the sixties and seventies on Scholastic Aptitude Test scores... before the decade is out."[87] But he was satisfied that "things are beginning to turn around."[88] In a rare instance, he cited his concern over "the problem of dropouts"—an equity agenda pushed back by excellence reform.[89] Overall, the Reagan radio talks further established Reagan's position as "teacher and preacher-in-chief" in education.

THE INFLUENCE OF WILLIAM J. BENNETT

Reagan kept the excellence reform movement alive in his choice of Bell's successor. In William J. Bennett, a former professor of philosophy and a former chairman of the National Endowment for the Humanities under Reagan, the president found the ideal "movement conservative" who would sustain the excellence reform movement. After Bennett resigned from the Department of Education shortly before the 1988 election, Reagan called him "the best thing to happen to American education since the McGuffey reader."[90]

Bennett ventured where angels feared to tread. Often with inflammatory language, he challenged every public education interest in his role as self-appointed guardian of conservative education values. He termed the movement to broaden university core courses in the humanities beyond the canon of white, male European authors nothing more than "nonsense" promoted by "trendy lightweights."[91] He criticized college and university faculties as political liberals who constituted "a threat . . . from the left and lost. . . . In shorthand, Marx and Marx brothers."[92] He attacked these university administrators for thriving on federal financial aid while each year substantially raising college tuitions beyond the reach of middle-class parents. He lambasted the Supreme Court for its "fastidious disdain for religion" and banning the use of public funds for parochial schools.[93] He condemned bilingual education as used by its adherents mainly to create cultural separateness, and he called for teaching English effectively. In short, Bennett confronted every controversial issue with a combination of half-truth and inflammatory logic concerning education in America.

To the public he represented extremes. One commentator characterized his role as preaching "a vaunted—and valuable—campaign for cultural and moral literacy. . . . [He] . . . was at his best campaigning around the country for higher educational standards."[94] For others Bennett merely indulged in a "narrow headline grabbing campaign."[95]

William Bennett also had an added dimension to his role in the Reagan White House. He became the point man in the Reagan revolution. One observer described him as "the administration's leading Reaganite . . . [who] . . . has transformed the Department of Education . . . into the last rampart of Reaganism."[96] Bennett perceived his function as a presidential loyalist who would be defender of the New Right's faith. For him, Ronald Reagan was a "great President," comparable to Lincoln.[97] Bennett often chided his fellow Reagan aides for not strongly supporting the president in the waning days of the second administration.

Bennett came to the Reagan White House by a now familiar route. He was part of a growing band of neoconservatives who supplied much of the intellectual firepower of the Reagan administration. Neoconservatives were described as conservatives who once were liberals or leftists. In his college years in the sixties, Bennett considered himself a "maverick" Democrat with New Left sympathies. At the time, he strongly favored the civil rights movement and opposed the Vietnam War.

With the advent of Black Power in the civil rights movement, Bennett as a Harvard Law School student in 1970 discarded his liberalism. Moreover, he strongly disliked the implicit anti-Americanism of some New Left leaders. It was not until 1987 that he formally became a member of the Republican party.

Bennett served two apprenticeships as a budding neoconservative. First, he studied philosophy at the University of Texas with John Silber, the controversial neoconservative who later became president of Boston University. Bennett became Silber's assistant at Boston University.

Later, Bennett made a more important neoconservative contact. He became a protégé of Irving Kristol, a founding father of neoconservatism, and editor of that group's key journal, *The Public Interest*. Kristol urged Reagan aides to appoint Bennett head of the National Endowment for the Humanities (NEH). Bennett rewarded his mentor by hiring Kristol's wife, the historian Gertrude Himmelfarb, on the NEH staff. Later Kristol's son, William, was hired by Bennett as his chief aide in the Department of Education.

Bennett politicized the National Endowment for the Humanities. He perceived his role as "defunding the culture of the New Left" and rejected proposals he felt revealed a "strong ideological bias highly critical of the government, the economic system . . . or a feminist perspective."[98] In turn, he and his chief aide for research in education, Chester E. Finn, Jr., were similarly accused of politicizing education research. For some of his sympathizers, Bennett was seen as having drifted too far right, having "accepted many of the core assumptions of the religious right," such as school prayer and vouchers for private and parochial schools, and identifying "religious education with moral education."[99]

One issue exemplifying Bennett's controversial style concerned attempts by younger scholars to revise the "literary canon" in core literature courses. The New Criticism of the 1940s and 1950s had established that a "canon" of outstanding literary works existed. Authors chosen for that canon were, according to the New Criticism, to be chosen on the basis of literary merit alone.

Younger literary scholars of the 1980s challenged the canon; they contended that it was restrictive. Overwhelmingly, authors included on the canon were white, male and either American or European. The younger scholars argued that the canon should be revised to include minority, women and non-European authors. They argued that such excluded writers should be listed for both literary and sociological reasons—the latter because of the need for literature to portray an era. A few elite universities, such as Stanford and Duke, began revising their literary reading lists along those lines. However, a Modern Language Association study in 1985 documented that an overwhelming number of undergraduate literature courses adhered to the old canon of writers.[100]

Bennett inflamed the controversy. In a major speech, he rather dogmatically condemned the revisionists in strong language:

Are we to labor to provide a good intellectual basis in high school only to pass students on to dopiness and trivialities in the halls of ivy? Serious voices are being drowned out by trendy lightweights in our midst. The clamor from these lightweights is giving higher education a bad name. And if their agenda is allowed to go unchecked and unchallenged, if at this moment in the academy's life its more responsible members choose to look away and avoid the struggle, higher education will be irreparably damaged.[101]

In turn, Bennett was roundly condemned by the younger scholars. Henry Louis Gates, Jr., a black professor at Cornell University, replied that "the process of canon reformation has always gone on" and in putting together the great White Western canon women and minorities were excluded.[102] Cary Nelson, a professor of English at the University of Illinois at Urbana, criticized Bennett for being "thoroughy dishonest" in implying that a revised canon "would eliminate the reading of classic texts."[103]

Stephen Graubard offered the most telling criticism of Bennett. A history professor at Brown University and editor of the prestigious journal *Daedelaus,* Graubard accused Bennett of misperceiving the problems of American higher education "by dwelling persistently and extensively on a few themes."[104] Graubard worte: "It is curious this kind of issue, so complex, which one would presume a distinguished faculty to be capable of dealing with, should figure so prominently in the Secretary's discourse when other issues, of greater urgency, go unmentioned."[105]

Bennett published informative studies and reports for the school practitioner. On the whole, these were useful treatises that summarized current research, were distributed primarily for teachers and administrators and were a laudatory attempt to close the gap between research and practice. Still, many of these well-documented reports had implications by Bennett that left much to be desired and were questionable interpretations of the data.

Let us examine Bennett's strength as a publisher of vital research. Perhaps his most moderate proposal was the curriculum he envisioned for his ideal high school. Dubbed James Madison High, Bennett's mythical school adhered to a core curriculum most suitable for the college bound. It was an extension of the curriculum advocated by the authors of *A Nation at Risk:* four years of English and three years, respectively, of math, science and social studies. In addition, Bennett added two years of both a foreign language and physical education and one year of fine arts.

Bennett's aim was cultural literacy. His core curriculum, in his view, would allow students "to take from high school a shared body of knowledge and skills, a common language of ideas, a common moral and intellectual discipline."[106] Although Bennett did not provide for a vocational track, he mentioned vocational courses, albeit in a minor key: "This document should

not be understood as an argument for the exclusion from high school curricula of special and vocational electives or substitutions. Indeed, in a number of places it notes the value of elective classes for continued supplemental
study.[107] The emphasis clearly is on the academic, college-bound track.

Bennett was equally equivocal when describing the role of his idealized
James Madison High School. He was quick to remind readers that this ideal
high school "is not a statement of federal policy."[108] For Bennett school
curricula were the province of states and localities; however, his role appeared to be that of key adviser so that James Madison High School should
serve "as a goal and ideal."[109]

Bennett also noted that many high schools had already approached the
James Madison ideal. He profiled six such public high schools. They are
representative: urban, suburban, rural and private. The other is a Catholic
high school in New Orleans—Xavier Prep.

The proposed curriculum for James Madison High School appeared to be
a sound grounding for the college bound. Nonetheless, this curriculum revealed the secretary of education's conservative cultural biases. The suggested syllabus for American literature reflected Bennett's adherence to the
New Criticism in literature. Of the American authors recommended only one
was a woman—Emily Dickinson—and only one was a black—Ralph Ellison.
None of the authors represented had published significant work after the
1950s.

The four-unit English track was comprehensive. In the ninth grade, students were introduced to literature from Homer to Shakespeare to Twain;
in the tenth grade, students were immersed in American literature; in the
eleventh grade, students studied British literature and in senior year, students
widened their perspective with world literature.

Bennett extended his version of a core curriculum into elementary school.
As his final publication as secretary, he proposed his ideal elementary
school—again named James Madison. This curriculum consisted of seven
parts: English, social studies, mathematics, science, foreign language, fine
arts and physical education/health.

For Bennett elementary education in the public schools of America left
much to be desired. He concluded that "the absolute level of American
elementary achievement is still too low" and that students still had "insuf-
ficient command of basic subjects."[110] Bennett's solution was for curriculum
reform. He failed to mention other reforms—in teaching administration or
finance to attract more capable teachers. He glossed over the "good news"
that the reading skills of students aged nine to thirteen had risen steadily
since the 1970s to a level termed by the National Assessment for Progress
"a considerable national achievement."[111]

Bennett's major changes, ironically, were in reading. He abhorred "English programs that spurn serious literature in favor of blank basal readers
and skill-work books"[112] Instead, Bennett proposed a mini–Great Books

program. That program would begin in kindergarten and continue through eighth grade. Bennett's selections represented some of the finest children's literature and the greatest books of the past. Some indicated contemporary themes and material once reserved for college. For example, selections for grades seven and eight included the contempoary black poet Mayo Angelou's autobiography, *I Know Why the Caged Bird Sings.* A more advanced text for eighth graders was Ernest Hemingway's parable *The Old Man and the Sea,* a text pursued in college literature courses a short generation ago.

A classic example of a soundly documented study published by the Department of Education with what critics perceived as interpretative excess by Bennett is *Japanese Education Today.* Since the excellence reform movement was triggered by Japanese economic success, it logically followed that policy makers would examine Japanese education.

The ninety-five-page report reviewed the literature on Japanese education; it placed strengths and weaknesses in context. In a section titled "Implications for American Education," Bennett clearly evinced worship of Japan. He concluded enviously that "Japanese education works."[113] Moreover, "our educational ideals are better realized on a large scale in Japan."[114]

Why did the Japanese succeed educationally? According to Bennett, it was because they posessed superior cultural values. He pointed out that "parental engagement ... makes a big difference"; that for students "motivation matters"; that schools successfully "transmit the shared and inherited culture" and that students possessed "sound character" and "take reponsibility."[115] The clear implication was that students, parents, teachers and administrators did not possess those values in America in sufficient quantity.

Critics quarreled with Bennett's assessment. For one thing, they pointed out that Bennett misinterpreted the data. The Japanese school system is highly deceptive, since it is buttressed by a network of private, profit-making schools, called Jukus, where the most motivated (and most affluent) continue schooling after hours each day. These Jukus prepare for the entry examinations to prestigious high schools and colleges. Jukus serve the purpose of preparing students for "examination hell." There are much less intensive preparation courses for SATs and professional entry examination in the United States, and the number of students in them is relatively small. In Japan, on the other hand, 47.3 percent of junior high school students in 1987 attended Jukus.[116] Thus, we have a public school system reinforcing a private school system.

For another thing, critics argued that the Japanese educational system is too culture-bound for foreign export. Harvard professor Merrie White in her book, *The Japanese Educational Challenge,* contended that the ethnic and cultural homogeneity of Japanese society makes that system a highly implausible alternative for the United States. For example, the authoritarian mores of the Japanese conflict with American democratic values.

Perhaps the key document of Bennett's tenure was his assessment of the excellence reform movement. Entitled *American Education: Making It Work,* Bennett's report card was issued five years after the publication of *A Nation at Risk.* Bennett's appraisal was self-congratulatory. He intoned: "The precipitous downward slide of previous decades has been arrested, and we have begun the long climb back to reasonable standards.... Our students have made modest gains in achievement...we are doing better than we were in 1983.... But we are certainly not doing well enough. We are still at risk."[117]

Once again, he repackaged the recommendations of *A Nation at Risk.* Bennett called for the establishment of a core curriculum in public schools, restoring order and discipline to create an "ethos of achievement" and merit pay for teachers.[118] He added the concept of choice in attending public schools, a variation of the voucher concept.

The secretary argued that current education research had found the answers to the problems of schooling. He concluded that teaching and learning were "not mysterious" and that "discovering what works—establishing the ideas and practices that make for effective schools—has been a signal achievement of the reform movement to date."[119]

Many scholars believed that although research had provided many clues to the mystery of learning, much was left to decipher, a problem not so much of researchers but of the nature of research in education itself with its many confounding variables. These scholars argued that it was one thing to assess experimental research in the laboratory; it was quite another matter to deal with people and the many factors that multiply.

Critics felt that Bennett was all too ready to accept the work of the effective school movement. First, they contended that effective schools research preceded the excellence reform movement; Rutter's key study, *Fifteen Thousand Hours,* was published in 1979 and examined schools in the early 1970s. Second, they argued that the research was primarily concerned with the disadvantaged and that the variables associated with effective schools may not necessarily be applied to more affluent student bodies. Third, these scholars pointed out that variables associated with effective schools, such as higher teacher expectations, are hard to operationalize into educational policy. Finally, they maintained that the body of effective research is still thin. Rutter's study was the major work done in England, and the work of a few American counterparts like Wilbur Brookover lacked the longitudinal base of the Rutter study.[120]

Effective school research remained attractive to both liberal and conservative policy makers. For the liberals, it was a sign of hope that poor children can be successfully educated. For conservatives such as Bennett, the elusive nature of the variables associated with effective schools was cost-free; there was no need for large infusions of money to implement in-service courses to sensitize teachers and administrators. For the Reagan administration such cost-free solutions to educational problems proved attractive.

Bennett collected his less controversial speeches in a book entitled *Our Children and Our Country*. What proved attractive to many educators was Bennett's concept of "moral literacy." He emphasized the need for schools and colleges to develop "the traits of character" in students that, for him, comprised moral literacy.[121] He defined moral literacy as the sensibility that will enable students "to make sense of what they will see in life, and, we may hope, will help them live it well."[122] Colleges, he intoned, have a responsibility to go beyond subject matter "to foster moral discernment in their students."[123]

For Bennett, moral literacy had a religious foundation. It was based on the "role of religion and the Judeo-Christian ethic in American democracy."[124] Moreover, its matrix was Western. For Bennett schools and colleges must "defend Western Civilization . . . because it is good. . . . The West has produced the world's most just and effective system of government: the system of representative democracy. . . . Western ideas remain still the last, best hope on earth.[125]

However, moral literacy in youngsters was endangered, according to Bennett, by the "decline of the American family," which "constitutes perhaps the greatest long-term threat to our children's well-being."[126] "The unavoidable answer" to the family's decline, he concluded, was self-help, help from the family itself—"individual mothers, individual fathers, individual families."[127]

The resurgence of conservatism in America had turned the moral tide. "American conservatism," he wrote, "now sets the terms of our national debate."[128] Most importantly, "on this moral and cultural front," he argued, "there are also grounds for new hope."[129] That new hope must be credited to President Reagan, whose moral dialogue, Bennett believed, constituted his most important achievement as president. Indeed, Bennett's collection of speeches set a calmer tone than his pronouncements as secretary of education and garnered praise from a number of educators, including S. Frederick Starr, president of Oberlin College:

To many, William J. Bennett . . . was the . . . motor-mouth of Maryland Avenue . . . with his gift for hyperbole, bombast, and, at times, outright silliness.

Such antics, to put it mildly, complicated the task of evaluating this collection of Bennett's speeches. . . .

[Yet] here is a public official who views education not as a means of developing the national pool of manpower or as a key to competitiveness, but as the sine qua non of individual fulfillment and the keystone to civic life in a representative democracy.[130]

For others—liberals and members of the educational establishment—William Bennett was a threat to public education. His introduction of a voucher plan for poor children, his reduced federal budgets submitted to Congress and his flaying away at the alleged sins of public educators alienated the education constituency. Mary Hatwood Futrell, president of the National Education Association, labeled Bennett's record on civil rights "less than exemplary."[131] The Democratic chairperson of the House Committee on Education and Labor, Augustus Hawkins, gave him a "failing grade."[132]

The moderately liberal editors of the New York Times rendered a negative report card on the third secretary of education. Calling him the "most memorable" of the three secretaries, they described his tenure as one in which "he gladly used his post as a pulpit . . . [where] . . . he was better at raising provocative questions than providing thoughtful answers [so that] . . . his tenure will be remembered more for polemics than education policy or planning."[133] In the end, he undermined President Reagan's desire to eliminate federal influence and the Department of Education "by serving him so well and raising the visibility of the Department . . . [which] . . . make that even harder."[134]

What did Bennett accomplish? For one thing, his brand of bully pulpit made him the best-known cabinet member. According to one journalist, he was "the most visible chief education officer the country has ever had."[135] In the process, he put the Department of Education on the map. One educator ironically credited Bennett for having "created what the liberals wanted."[136] Most importantly, he kept the focus on excellence school reform in the minds of the educational establishment, politicians and the American public.

Bennett departed the Reagan administration shortly before the end of Reagan's second term. Along with conservative philosopher Allan Bloom, author of the controversial and popular jeremiad The Closing of the American Mind, he formed an educational think tank called the Madison Center. This educational policy center continued excellence reform by having college undergraduates pursue a "great books" curriculum. Bennett's visibility and outspokenness on conservative ideology caused him to be in demand for political office. He was mentioned as a possible vice-presidential candidate for President Bush and as a senatorial candidate. He returned to the White House in 1989 as a presidential aide on drugs.

CHESTER E. FINN, JR.

While Bennett was the rhetorical point man in the Reagan administration, his chief aide, Chester E. Finn, Jr., provided the intellectual firepower. Before joining the Department of Education as assistant secretary for research in early 1985, Finn enjoyed a solid reputation as a scholar and educational policy aide. He served an apprenticeship as an educational policy adviser to President Nixon and as an aide to Daniel Patrick Moynihan, Nixon's chief urban affairs analyst. He then joined the liberal think tank, the Brookings Institution, as an education policy analyst. Later he became a professor of education and public policy at Vanderbilt University.

Finn's credentials as a scholar were impressive. He authored two books, coauthored another and coedited two more. In addition, he contributed a steady stream of articles to scholarly journals, most pressing for excellence school reform. Along with the historian Diane Ravitch, he cofounded the Education Excellence Network, which processed information on excellence reform. Finn left an indelible imprint in American educational history as the leading intellectual advocate for excellence school reform.

Following Bennett's example, Finn also became one of the most well-known aides in the Reagan administration. His chief governmental contribution was a series of publications—entitled *What Works*—that digested current research and interpreted research findings in lay language that could be used by the school practitioner—especially the American teacher.

Ironically, it was this Reagan education aide who forcefully argued in 1977 that the role of the president was limited in education. This conclusion was the result of his tenure in the Nixon administration.

Finn's interpretation was published as *Education and the Presidency*. This book was his doctoral dissertation at Harvard Graduate School of Education. As a dissertation and as a book it suffered from lack of organization and focus. Nonetheless, it was extremely valuable as a case study in presidential decision making. Moreover, Finn succinctly stated the case against presidential influence in education.

Finn argued that education is not a priority issue for several reasons. First, he argued that presidents concentrate almost wholly on foreign policy and national defense. Second, on domestic policy presidents "concentrate on issues where the federal role is dominant," and education "is ancillary to other national interests."[137] Third, he believed that "presidents see scant political reward for spending time on education."[138] Certainly, the latter two propositions have not stood the test of time. Yet, Finn is guilty of tunnel vision, as he based his observations on a president not greatly involved in education, such as Nixon, and neglected the large educational contribution of his predecessor, Lyndon Johnson.

Finn challenged the American educational research establishment. He accused educational researchers of pursuing the irrelevant. Consequently, Finn argued, the public associated educational research with "educational faddism on the one hand and pointy-headed intellectualism on the other."[139] The bottom line, Finn maintained, was that after two decades of extensive educational research, "our educational system has by many measures worsened."[140] Education research had had little impact on school practice, he argued: "Education research has not fulfilled its role in the effort to improve schools, perhaps because it runs into much skepticism from practitioners and policymakers. Hence, its effects are limited, and in turn fosters skepticism as to its potential—a wicked cycle."[141]

Although American educational research began to be more sophisticated with the federal infusionof grant money in the Johnson administration, very little of that research was policy-oriented. Finn made a harsh plea for research that had policy implications. Prior to the 1960s educational research was rather simple, usually descriptive and relying on surveys. Eventually, it developed experimental and, later, qualitative research. However, the trend toward policy studies was only a recent development.

Understandably, the American research establishment was defensive. Richard J. Shavelson, president of the American Educational Research Association (AERA), and David C. Berliner, past president, replied that Finn "misrepresents education research's contribution to educational improvement."[142] Somewhat disingenuously, these researchers pointed to the policy implications of effective school research, which had been routinely dismissed by AERA journal authors as being weak because of its qualitative component. They contended: "Substantively, for example, the effective school research has had a profound influence on the school systems across the country. The eight concepts underlying effective schools...have given school systems a set of goals to work for: a sense of mission."[143]

More importantly, congressional critics criticized as politicized the awarding of research grants during Finn's tenure. Researchers with a conservative ideological bent were favored. One congressional aide concluded that "Finn has failed to convince the powers that be up here that what he is proposing is in the best interest of education in this country."[144]

Along with the historican Diane Ravitch, Finn collaborated on a study published for popular consumption as a book about student achievement during his tenure at the Department of Education. This study was an assessment of high school students' knowledge of literature and history. It was conducted jointly by the National Assessment of Progress and the Finn-Ravitch Educational Excellence Network.

The assessment consisted of two separate tests administered to a sample of 8,000 seventeen-year-old high school students. The sample was drawn from every representative area in America from urban to rural to suburban and answered 141 questions in history and 121 questions in literature. Of these students in the sample, fully 78 percent had taken United States history in the first year of high school.[145]

The results were unclear. The study revealed that 54.5 percent of the history answers were correct; in literature, 51.8 percent of the answers were correct.[146] Ravitch and Finn perceived the glass half empty rather than half full. They concluded that the "results...show that while a few students did well, most did not perform satisfactorily."[147] However, since no such national tests had been given in the past, one lacked a benchmark for comparison. Were our parents or grandparents more knowledgeable? Indeed, the authors hedged and stated that "we do not assert that American youth know less about the past than their predecessors."[148]

Indeed, the study was criticized on those grounds. Stephen Graubard wrote that Finn and Ravitch were "new Cassandras ... alarmist critics who cry Beowulf."[149] He seriously questioned the usefulness of the study. Moreover, he doubted whether "our aging political leaders, all educated in that glorious era before 1945 ... so fondly and nostalgically recalled" would pass the tests.[150] "One wonders what the results would be if the President and all his cabinet members were invited to write a handful of sentences on [the tests] ... thereby demonstrating their literary competence. Would the 'class' do well, or would we be appalled by the results?"[151]

The authors noted the neglect of core history and literature courses in favor of bland survey courses. Such generic blocks as "social studies" and "language arts," they argued, diluted academic programs. What had happened was an educational "sleight of hand," whereby a weak course such as marriage and the family might be substituted for a traditional history course. The authors argued for a traditional core curriculum that would provide a "modicum of coherence."[152]

The results of their study disappointed Finn and Ravitch in one significant respect. Although both were perhaps the leading intellectual advocates of excellence reform, they felt that policy makers were too intent on programming curricula that had an economic potential. They observed that policy makers were all too eager to strengthen mathematics and science courses because these subjects "had utilitarian value ... [being] ... linked directly to jobs and careers."[153] On the other hand, the advocates for emphasizing such liberal arts courses as history and literature were few.

The authors offered educators a series of broad recommendations to correct that neglect. These included such items as devoting more time to the teaching of history, requiring two years of world history and reintroducing chronology and geography. For literature, they recommended more time in the study of literature and providing a "coherent" core curriculum, a "canon" of "works that have received some degree of recognition for their quality."[154]

Finally, Finn and Ravitch had advice for policy makers. They urged that a core curriculum be re-established in the high schools in America with a prominent place reserved for history and literature. They advised that the teachers of such courses must be knowledgeable even if that goal meant bypassing graduates of schools of education for other graduates with those majors.

THE IMPACT OF EXCELLENCE REFORM

What has been the impact of the excellence reform movement on the schools? It appears to have been mixed. At first glance, the excellence reform movement seems to have been a moderate success. Five years after *A Nation at Risk* was released, more than 220,000 copies were distributed by the

Department of Education and an estimated 5 to 6 million copies were distributed through newspaper and magazine reprints, including foreign translations.[155] The states appeared to respond to the challenge. By spring 1988, all but five states had raised high school graduation requirements. Over two dozen had made educational improvements ranging from higher teacher salaries to new discipline codes.[156]

Indeed, Bennett could cite positive effects of excellence reform. Five years after *A Nation at Risk,* in all but two of the fifty states, education was the single largest budget item.[157] SAT scores had gained a few points since 1980 and stabilized. Modest gains were also recorded in reading and writing. Math scores also improved incrementally, and science students had made up lost ground.[158]

The excellence school reform movement was more profound than past educational fads. Indeed, education reformers described successive "waves" of the movement. The first wave saw state legislatures raising academic standards and teacher salaries. The second wave saw school administrators revising curriculum and teacher training. A third wave has been called for by educational reformers to restructure education fundamentally, specifically to enlarge the federal role, a position vigorously rebuffed by Secretary of Education William Bennett, who said that he "didn't think the federal role had to be brought into the conversation."[159]

However, the first systematic study of the impact of excellence reform indicated that much of the upgrading of the schools had taken place before *A Nation at Risk* was released. In a study commissioned by the prestigious educational journal *Phi Delta Kappan,* William W. Wayson and associates concluded that the "largest proportion of" reform activities reported had been initiated before May 1983.[160] These included adding computer literacy courses, increasing requirements in math, science and English, offering foreign languages to elementary students and increasing homework. After *A Nation at Risk* was published, these districts increased science graduation requirements and continued to raise math standards, require foreign languages and English and require homework. Wayson studied fifty-nine school districts of exemplary nature selected by the fifty state education departments. All but two states nominated at least one district.

School administrators in these model school districts did perceive some negative fallout from excellence school reform, which was seen as having "given excessive importance to standardized testing . . . [so that] . . . the effective and creative dimension of the curriculum . . . [is neglected, thus] . . . undermining the attainment of higher-level thinking skills."[161] Equally importantly, these educators feared an erosion of local authority as states asserted increasing authority in education. Finally, the school people were upset that the excellence reform movement gave the public a negative view of the schools.

The excellence reform movement had some significant policy impacts.

First, it once again made education a national issue. Second, excellence reform shifted the policy focus from the disadvantaged, where it had been since Johnson's Great Society, to the education of the best and brightest. Third, excellence reform redirected educational influence from the federal government to the states. Fourth, attention was switched from the elementary schools, where equity interventions are most plausible, to high schools, where final academic grooming begins.

NOTES

1. Paul Kennedy, *The Rise and Fall of the Great Powers: Economic Change and Military Conflict from 1500 to 2000* (New York: Random House, 1987), p. 515.

2. Ibid., p. 521.

3. Ibid., pp. 514-15.

4. Benjamin M. Friedman, *Day of Reckoning: The Consequences of American Economic Policy Under Reagan and After* (New York: Random House, 1988), p. 4.

5. Ibid., p. 19.

6. Ibid., p. 13.

7. Ibid., p. 51.

8. Ibid.

9. Ibid., p. 28.

10. Ibid., p. 6.

11. Ibid., p. 39.

12. Ibid.

13. Deborah A. Verstegen and David L. Clark, "The Diminution in Federal Expenditures for Education During the Reagan Administration," *Phi Delta Kappan,* October 1988, p. 135.

14. Ibid., pp. 134-35.

15. Ibid.

16. Ibid., p. 138.

17. Ibid.

18. Ibid.

19. Ibid.

20. Ronald Reagan (with Richard G. Hubler), *Where's the Rest of Me?* (New York: Karz, 1965), p. 7.

21. Ibid., pp. 9-10.

22. Ibid., p. 10.

23. Ibid., p. 24.

24. Ibid.

25. Ibid., p. 30.

26. Ronald Reagan, *The Creative Society* (New York: Devin-Adair, 1968), p. 125.

27. Ibid.

28. Ibid., p. 120.

29. Ibid.

30. Ibid., p. 122.

31. Martin Smith, "Lessons from the California Experience," *Change*, September 1980, p. 33.

32. Ibid., p. 32.

33. Ibid., p. 37.

34. Ibid.

35. Shirley Boes Neill, "The Reagan Education Record in California," *Phi Delta Kappan*, October 1989, p. 137.

36. Ibid.

37. Richard F. Elmore and Milbrey Wallin McLaughin, *Reform and Retrenchment: The Politics of California School Finance Reform* (Cambridge, Mass.: Ballinger, 1982), p. 92.

38. Terrel H. Bell, *The Thirteenth Man: A Reagan Cabinet Memoir* (New York: Free Press, 1988), p. 123.

39. Ibid.

40. U.S. Department of Education, *A Nation at Risk: The Imperative for Educational Reform* (Washington, D.C.: U.S. Government Printing Office, 1983), p. 5.

41. *New York Times*, April 27, 1988, p. B.10.

42. Ibid.

43. Ibid.

44. Lawrence C. Steadman and Marshall S. Smith, "Weak Arguments, Poor Data, Simplistic Recommendations," in *The Great School Debate*, ed. Beatrice and Ronald Gross (New York: Simon and Schuster, 1985), p. 88.

45. Ronald Reagan, "The President's Address to the National Forum on Excellence in Education," *American Education*, March 1983, p. 2.

46. Bell, *The Thirteenth Man*, p. 127.

47. Ibid.

48. Maurice R. Berube, "Education and the Poor," *Commonweal*, March 31, 1967, p. 46.

49. Diane Ravitch, *The Troubled Crusade: American Education, 1945–1980* (New York: Basic Books, 1983), p. xii.

50. Ronald Reagan, "The President's Radio Address to the Nation on Education," *American Education*, May 1983, p. 2.

51. Ibid.

52. Reagan, "The President's Address," p. 3.

53. Bell, *The Thirteenth Man*, p. 9.

54. Ibid., p. 12.

55. Ibid., p. 2.

56. Ibid.

57. Ibid., p. 3.

58. Ibid., p. 36.

59. Ibid., p. 22.

60. Ibid., p. 163.

61. Ibid., p. 116.

62. Ibid.

63. Ibid.

64. Ibid., p. 161.

65. Ibid., p. 153.

66. Hugh Sidey, "School Days, Then and Now," *Time*, July 11, 1983, p. 16.

67. *Time*, June 20, 1983, p. 14.

68. Ibid.

69. Bell, *The Thirteenth Man*, p. 159.

70. Ronald Reagan, "State of the Union: 1983," *Vital Speeches of the Day*, February 15, 1983, p. 260.

71. Ibid., pp. 260-61.

72. Ronald Reagan, "State of the Union: 1984," *New York Times*, January 26, 1984.

73. Ronald Reagan, "State of the Union: 1985," *New York Times*, February 7, 1985, p. 38.

74. Ibid.

75. Ronald Reagan, "State of the Union: 1986," *New York Times*, February 5, 1986, p. A.20.

76. Ibid.

77. Ronald Reagan, "State of the Union: 1988," *New York Times*, January 26, 1988, p. A.16.

78. Ronald Reagan, "Address to the Republican Party National Convention," *New York Times*, August 16, 1988, p. A.20.

79. Ronald Reagan, *Ronald Reagan's Weekly Radio Addresses: The President Speaks to America, Vol. 1: The First Term*, compiled by Fred L. Israel (Wilmington, Del.: Scholarly Resources, Inc., 1987), p. 82.

80. Ibid., p. 97.

81. Ibid.

82. Ibid., p. 98.

83. Ibid.

84. Ibid., p. 209.

85. Ibid., p. 210.

86. Ibid., p. 243.

87. Ibid.

88. Ibid., p. 242.

89. Ibid., p. 243.

90. *New York Times*, August 10, 1988, p. A.12.

91. *Chronicle of Higher Education*, February 17, 1988, p. A.16.

92. *Virginian Ledger-Star*, April 11, 1986, p. A.10.

93. *Time*, July 18, 1988, p. 60.

94. John B. Judis, "Mister ED," *New Republic*, April 27, 1987, pp. 17-18.

95. Ibid., p. 16.

96. Ibid.

97. Ibid.

98. Judis, "Mister ED," p. 17.

99. Ibid., p. 18.

100. *Chronicle of Higher Education*, February 17, 1988, p. A.16.

101. Ibid.

102. Ibid., p. 1.

103. Ibid.

104. Stephen R. Graubard, "Education Secretary Bennett Misperceives the Prob-

lems of American Higher Education," *Chronicle of Higher Education,* March 16, 1988, p. A52.

105. Ibid.

106. William J. Bennett, *James Madison High School* (Washington, D.C.: U.S. Department of Education, December 1987), p. 4.

107. Ibid., p. 2.

108. Ibid., p. 3.

109. Ibid.

110. William J. Bennett, *James Madison Elementary School* (Washington, D.C.: U.S. Department of Education, August 1988), p. 2.

111. Ibid., p. 13.

112. Ibid., p. 4.

113. U.S. Department of Education, *Japanese Education Today* (Washington, D.C.: U.S. Government Printing Office, January 1987), p. 69.

114. Ibid.

115. Ibid., pp. 69-71.

116. Ibid., p. 11.

117. William J. Bennett, *American Education: Making It Work* (Washington, D.C.: U.S. Department of Education, April 1988), p. 1.

118. Ibid., p. 35.

119. Ibid., p. 2.

120. Maurice R. Berube, *Education and Poverty: Effective Schooling in the United States and Cuba* (Westport, Conn.: Greenwood Press, 1984).

121. William J. Bennett, *Our Children and Our Country: Improving America's Schools and Affirming the Common Culture* (New York: Simon and Schuster, 1988), p. 79.

122. Ibid.

123. Ibid., p. 140.

124. Ibid., p. 168.

125. Ibid., pp. 195-201.

126. Ibid., p. 64.

127. Ibid., p. 65.

128. Ibid., p. 227.

129. Ibid., p. 229.

130. S. Frederick Starr, review of William J. Bennett's *Our Children and Our Country, Washington Post,* October 18, 1988, p. D.3.

131. *Time,* July 18, 1988, p. 60.

132. Ibid.

133. *New York Times,* August 13, 1980, p. 26.

134. Ibid.

135. *New York Times,* September 18, 1988, p. 26.

136. Ibid.

137. Chester E. Finn, Jr., *Education and the Presidency* (Lexington, Mass.: Lexington Books, 1977), pp. 103-4.

138. Ibid.

139. Chester E. Finn, Jr., "What Ails Education Research," *Educational Research,* January-February 1988, p. 5.

140. Ibid.

141. Ibid.

142. Richard J. Shavelson and David C. Berliner, "Erosion of the Education Research Infrastructure," *Educational Research,* January-February 1988, p. 9.

143. Ibid.

144. Robin Wilson, "Education Department Official in Charge of Research Thrives on Controversy While Seeking to Bolster Field," *Chronicle of Higher Education,* November 23, 1987, p. A.22.

145. Diane Ravitch and Chester E. Finn, Jr., *What Do Our 17 Year Olds Know? A Report on the First National Assessment of History and Literature* (New York: Harper and Row, 1987), p. 46.

146. Ibid., pp. 46, 85.

147. Ibid., p. ix.

148. Ibid., p. 200.

149. Stephen R. Graubard, "Alarmist Critics Who Cry Beowulf," *New York Times,* October 1, 1987, p. A.27.

150. Ibid.

151. Ibid.

152. Ravitch and Finn, *What Do Our 17 Year Olds Know?,* p. 9.

153. Ibid., p. 14.

154. Ibid., p. 15.

155. Edward B. Fiske, "35 Pages that Shook the U.S. Education World," *New York Times,* April 27, 1988, p. B.10.

156. Ibid.

157. Bennett, *American Education: Making It Work,* p. 7.

158. Ibid., pp. 7-30.

159. Fiske, *New York Times,* April 27, 1988, p. B. 10.

160. William W. Wayson et al., *Up from Excellence: The Impact of the Excellence Movement on the Schools* (Bloomington, Ind.: Phi Delta Kappa Foundation, 1988), p. 121.

161. Ibid., pp. 138-39.

6

George Bush (1989–   ) and National Standards

President George Bush inherited the educational agenda of his predecessor, Ronald Reagan. Bush was determined to continue the excellence reform movement begun in the Reagan White House.

There was little in Bush's background that would justify his calling himself an education president. Still, he managed to continue the thrust of excellence reform through a bully pulpit and added a new dimension of his own in the advocacy of choice programs for the schools.

For the most part, Bush, like Reagan, practiced an educational politics of the bully pulpit. He declared that, for him, educational leadership would be mainly "hortatory."[1] Like Reagan, he perceived education to be a responsibility of the states, with the role of the federal government to suggest a national agenda for the states. Consequently, his educational budgets were minimal and prompted the educational establishment to brand them "lackluster."[2]

Nevertheless, Bush's contribution to excellence reform was significant. First, he called an educational summit of all the governors to establish national educational goals. Second, he shaped the national educational agenda through his strong emphasis on choice plans. Choice meant that students would be permitted to attend any school they desired. Choice was an idea that was easily compressible and attractive to parents, students and politicians in search of no-cost solutions.

The purpose of Bush's continuation of excellence reform was, of course, to regain America's economic competitive strength. In his messages and his actions, the American economy was in the background of all education reform.

We shall examine Bush's educational initiatives in greater detail. First, the

1988 presidential campaign will be analyzed. For the first time in American history, education became a theme of all candidates in both major parties. The 1988 presidential campaign may have signaled a major shift in national educational politics.

CASE STUDY: THE 1988 PRESIDENTIAL CAMPAIGN

The economic scenario had substantially changed American educational politics. By 1988, no presidential candidate could afford to neglect education as a campaign issue. How committed and how serious these candidates were in addressing the educational issue were questionable. What was not debatable, however, was that education as a national concern had finally reached a presidential level.

For the first time, education became a bipartisan issue. Formerly, it was terrain mainly occupied by the Democrats. Edward B. Fiske, the *New York Times* education correspondent, noted that "Democrats have pretty much had the education issue to themselves... [a situation that put] the Democrats, who were committed to expand educational opportunities on the offensive and the Republicans, committed to fiscal restraint on the defensive."[3] The excellence reform movement of the 1980s changed all that. In the 1988 campaign all seven of the Democratic candidates and all six of the Republican candidates emphasized education as a priority.

Among these presidential aspirants in 1988 there was neither consensus nor a clear image regarding education. The Republican nominee, George Bush, for example, "didn't quite know what he meant," according to his chief education adviser, when he said that he wanted to be known as "the education president."[4] His commitment was a vague calling for improvement in the nation's schools and colleges. One Democratic contender, former governor Bruce Babbitt, claimed the "children issue" and proposed a new cabinet Office of the Child with a woman in charge dispensing a national system of child-care vouchers to the states.

The education platforms of the candidates ran the gamut in both variety and intensity. Strategies ranged from such excellence reform issues as raising teacher and student standards to the old equity agenda of more aid for the disadvantaged through literacy programs. All the candidates sensed the importance of education as an issue, and rode the crest of the excellence reform movement, but none seemed to be able to develop an agenda that would capture the attention of the public. The difficulty was in translating educational ideas into votes.

Let us examine the education platforms of the six Republican candidates and the seven Democrats in the primaries. We will focus more closely on the two presidential candidates selected by their parties.

In the Republican primaries, the other five candidates besides George Bush echoed much of the Reagan education program. Senator Bob Dole mainly repackaged excellence reform issues. He argued for raising teacher and student standards. Some of Dole's aides confided that Dole "has not thought deeply about the issues" in education.[5] During the campaign he said little about education. Alexander Haig, Jr., former secretary of state in the Reagan administration, echoed the aims of the excellence reform movement. He asked for higher student standards and emphasized that teachers should "teach virtues, not just values."[6]

Pete Du Pont, heir to the chemical fortune, was the strongest advocate for a voucher program that would include federal monies for private and parochial schools in addition to public schools. Pat Robertson, the fundamentalist minister, reiterated the call for vouchers and stressed also school prayer in the public schools. He advocated merit pay and the elimination of progressive education in the schools. Congressman Jack Kemp argued for a variation of the voucher plan—freedom of choice in selecting public schools. Moreover, he called for tuition tax credits to shore up private and parochial education; however, he opposed vouchers on the grounds that they would "interfere with the commitment to public education."[7]

On the other hand, the Democratic candidates other than Governor Dukakis emphasized the old equity agenda. Congressman Richard Gephardt sought universal literacy. Former Senator Gary Hart and Senator Albert Gore, Jr., also made literacy a campaign pledge. Both civil rights leader Jesse Jackson and Senator Paul Simon called for more money for schools. Jackson proclaimed the right to college; he argued that "higher education must be seen as a right, and not a privilege, in our nation."[8] Senator Paul Simon called for higher salaries for teachers, literacy programs and more grants for college students—what one journalist termed "vintage Democratic ideas.[9]

Former governor Bruce Babbitt campaigned on a blend of Democratic and Republican ideas in education. On the one hand, he proposed a new cabinet Office of the Child with a woman at the helm. On the other hand, he proposed child-care vouchers.

One can perceive two distinct partisan themes. For the most part, Republicans advocated no-cost solutions; moreover, they favored shoring up private and parochial schools. On the other hand, Democrats emphasized some spending programs and the education of the disadvantaged. One Democratic candidate revived the old Harry Truman idea of the right to college. Later we will examine more closely and in greater detail the two nominees of their parties, Michael Dukakis and George Bush.

Most educational critics gave the candidates low marks. John Goodlad, one of the nation's leading educators, described the educational issues raised by the candidates as "flimsy."[10] College presidents described the 1988 presidential race as one in which the candidates "failed to talk meaningfully about the issue [of education]."[11] A seasoned educational presidential watcher was harsher: "Most of the 14 presidential aspirants who took part singled out education as a high, even nonnegotiable, priority. But the skimpy knowledge and stale viewpoints they demonstrated did little to advance their candidates in pro-education circles."[12]

Part of that problem could be attributed to the candidates' political aides, who had yet to appreciate education as the strong issue public polls had indicated. One conservative political analyst pessimistically concluded that "education in 1988 could be what terrorism was in 1984: something the people talk about that doesn't change many votes."[13] A Democratic party pollster shared the same skepticism; he categorized education as "a good issue" but, nonetheless, one that doesn't "decide the next president."[14] The American media could be faulted for not fully recognizing the political import of education. Still, for the first time education was on the national presidential campaign priority list.

Both presidential nominees recognized education's political value in the campaign. Vice-President Bush not only called himself an education president but considered education "our most powerful economic program."[15] Not to be outdone, Michael Dukakis proclaimed that the "President of the United States becomes this nation's number one advocate for educational opportunity, good teaching, and good schools."[16]

The candidates issued position papers, party platforms and educational rhetoric. On balance, few of the educational issues captured the attention of the public; however, each candidate raised educational issues that did have noteworthy effect. Michael Dukakis' controversial college loan proposal, issued halfway through the campaign, provoked considerable discussion, and President Bush's espousal of the choice plan became an extremely galvanizing issue after the election.

The position papers varied in length and complexity. Vice-President Bush distributed a terse, one-page policy statement, whereas Governor Dukakis issued an eight-page statement blending proposals and criticism of the Reagan administration's educational policies.

As could be expected, both party candidates parted company on educational philosophy and strategy. Bush placed the focus on state and local spending and less federal intervention. He called for higher academic standards and a value base curriculum with emphasis on school dicipline and parent participation.

Dukakis castigated the Reagan government for cutting federal education programs by as much as 16 percent.[17] He proposed some spending proposals, such as a federally funded National Teaching Excellence Fund, which would forgive college loans for prospective teachers, increase literacy programs and guarantee the "right to college" through his loan program.

However, in his acceptance speech at the Democratic party convention Dukakis barely mentioned education. Instead, he echoed the style and substance of John F. Kennedy. His theme was "a time for wonderful new beginnings...a new era of greatness for America."[18] He called for a voluntary education program: "I want students and office workers and retired teachers to share with a neighbor the precious gift of literacy."[19]

In an equally optimistic vein, Bush accepted the Republican party nomination one month later. He promised to "keep America moving forward."[20] His theme contended that "America was not in decline" but "a rising nation."[21] The vice-president congratulated the Reagan-Bush administration on "economic growth ... [which] is the key to our endeavors."[22] Consequently, his education message was muted.

He did reiterate the substance of the excellence school reform movement of the 1980s. He proclaimed that "every one of our children deserves a first-rate school."[23] He wanted to see "power in the hands of the parents."[24] Moreover, he would encourage merit schools and increase federal funding for Head Start programs.

Neither Bush's nor Dukakis' remarks on education in his acceptance speech were extended. Dukakis devoted less than 50 words to education in a speech that was approximately 3,000 words in length. The Bush ratio was approximately the same.

The party platforms signaled few bold education initiatives. Only Bush's concept of choice—in which students attend public schools of their preference—had promise of stirring the educational waters.

Dukakis wanted to pursue no-cost solutions in order to redress the federal budget deficit in the best way. However, he was outmaneuvered by his main primary rival, Jesse Jackson. Jackson wanted to double federal spending on education. The issue was destined for a convention floor fight. Other volatile Jackson demands—Palestinian self-determination and a freeze on military spending—forced a compromise, and education spending was increased.

However, the education compromise failed to satisfy fully either the Dukakis or Jackson forces. The other politically explosive issues were dropped, and a tame pledge to increase "federal funding for education ... to better balance our priorities" was adopted.[25]

Only about 200 words were devoted in the Democratic party platform to education. The usual bland rhetoric was employed, enunciating that "the education of our citizens ... deserves our highest priority" and that "history will judge the next administration ... by its success in improving young minds."[26] The only new idea was the endorsement of a "principle that one should not be denied the opportunity to attend college for financial reasons."[27] This latter concept was a precursor to the Dukakis STARS college loan program, which he developed by midcampaign.

The Republicans had more ringing rhetoric and extended remarks. Their platform consisted of some 700 words—triple that of the Democratic statement—and was more precise and better written. Part of the reason that it was longer was that the platform writers felt compelled to stress the accomplishments of the Reagan-Bush administration in education. They gloated:

Republican leadership has launched a new era in American education. Our vision of excellence has brought education back to parents, back to basics, and back on a track of excellence leading to a brighter and stronger future for America....

We kept the spotlight on the reform movement through White House leadership, and we refocused the Department of Education to recognize and foster excellence.[28]

The Bush party platform continued discussing reform issues. It called for an expansion of the curriculum to include history, culture and geography; in addition, performance testing of both teachers and students was urged.

The new Bush idea was choice, which we will examine in more detail later. The platform proclaimed that "choice in education, especially for poor familes, fosters the parental involvement that is essential for school success."[29]

In the two presidential and one vice-presidential debates education did not figure prominently, due, in part, to their format, in which journalists asked prepared questions. None of the journalists specifically asked a question on education; consequently, the candidates mentioned education only parenthetically. This fact may be an indication of how little the media considered education a campaign issue.

In the first presidential debate, Governor Dukakis stressed his college loan program. In addition, he criticized the cuts in federal education spending by the Reagan-Bush administration. Bush responded by denying that the previous administration had reduced federal education spending.

Education was mentioned in the second debate only when the candidates were asked to mention their personal heroes. Responding first, Dukakis spoke of "classroom teachers I have had, classroom teachers that youngsters have today who are real heroes to our young people because they inspire them."[30] Bush mentioned a teacher who was the subject of a Hollywood film, "a teacher right here...Jaime Escalante, teaching calculus to young kids, 80 percent of them going to college."[31]

Neither did the vice-presidential debate promote education. The Republican nominee, Senator Dan Quayle, must be given good marks for trying. In his opening statement, he began the debate by listing "three issues" on his national agenda: "national security and arms control, jobs and education, and the Federal budget deficit."[32] However, before he could expand on these topics, the focus of the debate shifted to Senator Quayle's qualifications should he become president in an emergency.

In early September, almost two months after the Democratic party convention, Michael Dukakis presented his college loan plan. The plan was given the acronym STARS for Student Tuition and Repayment System. The purpose of the plan was to guarantee that every student could afford a college education, even at an expensive, elite private university. Dukakis' college loan plan enabled the candidate to take the initiative in the education debate. It was widely discussed by educators, the media and concerned citizens; however, it was highly controversial.

The plan entailed a complicated formula that, in effect, would have college graduates with higher paying jobs subsidizing the education of graduates with lower paying jobs. The plan offered no new federal monies but offered federal backing for loans at market rates of interest obtained from private banks. Repayment of the loans would be based on a flat percentage of a graduate's income. Graduates who earned more would pay more altogether than graduates who earned less.

Supporters of the college loan plan perceived three main advantages. First, the Dukakis plan would enable anyone who could be admitted to a college to attend regardless of family income. Second, it would allow students to choose elite private universities. Third, students might be permitted to choose service—but low-paid—occupations such as teaching without undue financial burden.

Supporters comprised educational and political liberals and, naturally, presidents of private colleges. The *New York Times* strongly endorsed the STARS program as "a presidential idea."[33] The newspaper editorialist pointed out that "collection would be as simple as Social Security deductions—unlike the huge defaults by students in the present unwieldy guaranteed Federal Loan Program."[34] Moreover the *Times* noted that "expensive private colleges would become plausible alternatives."[35] The *Times* concluded that "the plan embodies a laudable view of the role of government . . . using innovation and minimal intervention in the economy."[36] The president of the National Association of Independent Colleges and Universities strongly endorsed "the income contingency loan."[37]

Critics, including partisan Republican critics and financiers, scored the financial weaknesses in the STARS program. The Reagan administration was quick to attack the subsidization concept of lower earning graduates. Bruce M. Carnes, deputy secretary of education, predicted that the plan "won't work because it is based on the theory of redistribution of wealth."[38] Carnes contended that any student who wants to attend college may do so under current federal loan programs. He characterized the Dukakis plan as "a solution in search of a problem," a loan that never ends.[39] Most importantly, Carnes believed that the STARS program was doomed to failure because it was unlikely that students who could earn large amounts of money would participate. And without potential higher earners to participate there would not be sufficient monies to subsidize potential lower earners.

Some financiers found the long-term costs of STARS to be exorbitant. Two consumer finance writers, Jeff Blysdal and Marie Hodge, estimated that a student could pay as much as $55,000 in interest over twenty years on an $8,000 loan.[40] They concluded that "any youngster in this country qualified to do college work—including mathematics—should quickly see the financial peril of becoming STARS-struck."[41] They reiterated Carnes' contention that the necessary "support for needy and not-so-needy students is out there."[42]

The STARS plan was a bold initiative that temporarily captured the education offensive for Governor Dukakis; however, it was not fully thought out. Its greatest strength—access to expensive, elite universities—was also its greatest drawback. It was questionable to some that the government should shore up private schooling at the expense of public higher education.

GEORGE BUSH'S BACKGROUND

George Bush was born to wealthy parents. One of five children, he inherited money from both sides of his family. His father had amassed a fortune in investment banking, reorganizing failing companies. On his mother's side, Bush's grandfather had become wealthy in oil development.

In addition, Bush had a political model in his father. After becoming wealthy, Bush's father entered politics in liberal Connecticut during the popular election of Dwight D. Eisenhower. Bush described his father as a "conservative Republican...lined up with...the Eisenhower wing of the party."[43] His father lost a close election for U.S. senator in 1950. However, he was appointed to fill the unexpired term of the deceased senator Brien McMahon and was elected in 1952 and served ten years in the U.S. Senate.

George Bush was to follow in his family's footsteps, both in amassing wealth and in obtaining political success. Before attending Yale University, he served in the navy as a pilot during World War II. He had a distinguished naval tour of duty, completed fifty-eight combat missions and was shot down. He attended Yale, completed his academic work in two and one-half years—not uncommon for returning veterans—and earned Phi Beta Kappa.

Bush followed his maternal grandfather into the oil business and was also successful. He entered Texas politics as a moderate Republican and was elected in 1966 to the U.S. Congress. Four years later, he lost to Lloyd Bentsen in a campaign for the U.S. Senate. President Nixon thereupon appointed him U.S. ambassador to the United Nations, and President Ford selected him as director of the Central Intelligence Agency.

Bush campaigned for the Republican nomination for president in 1980, making a strong bid but eventually losing to Ronald Reagan. In the process, he called Reagan's economic program "voodoo economics," a phrase that would haunt him in 1988.[44] Reagan selected the moderate Bush as his vice-presidential running mate to balance the ticket.

George Bush placed no special value on the merits of education. He had attended elite Eastern boarding schools and an elite Eastern university and, in the opinion of one close observer, had developed the "patrician sensibility" of his class.[45] He was a mediocre student at Phillips Academy in

Massachusetts, but after having matured in the war, he was a good one at Yale. At Yale he majored in economics and minored in sociology.

In his memoirs published before the 1988 campaign, *Looking Forward,* there was scant mention of education. He devoted but a short paragraph to the subject and mainly commented that he "didn't find [economics] dismal at all."[46] In summing up his academic experience, he concluded that "he enjoyed the work, studied hard, [and] did well enough in his class to earn Phi Beta Kappa and other honors."[47]

According to his memoirs, his real interest was athletics. He devoted more space in the book to sports than academics, and he wrote that his "real minor" in college "as far as my attention span went, [was] soccer and baseball . . . especially baseball."[48]

One critic questioned Bush's intellectual proclivity. Journalist Gail Sheehy, interviewing Bush during the 1988 campaign, observed that "clearly, Bush is not fired up by ideas."[49] The key for Sheehy was that "Bush cannot remember a single book that influenced him."[50]

THE EDUCATION SUMMIT

Perhaps President Bush's most serious gambit as an education president was to call an education summit of all fifty governors in September 1989 at Charlottesville, Virginia. It was only the third time in American history that such a summit had been called by a president. Theodore Roosevelt had called one to establish conservation policy, and Franklin Delano Roosevelt had called one to respond to the Great Depression.[51] The summit was a powerful signal that education was a national concern in the wake of a crisis in international economic competition.

The purpose of the summit was clear. A joint statement by the president and the governors declared that the meeting was "to establish clear, national performance goals . . . that will make us internationally competitive."[52] In order to prepare for the summit, Bush sought the best thinking from education experts. Bush met "with every conceivable education group" in Washington, according to one observer, and the governors considered "hastily prepared papers" reflecting how some of the "experts could produce . . . about how the schools should be reformed."[53]

Nevertheless, the education summit conveyed mixed signals from the newest education president. According to aides, the president chose the University of Virginia for the summit, not Washington, D.C., "to avoid any suggestion that education is a national responsibility—and thus something requiring lots of money."[54] Indeed, Bush declared at the summit that "our goals must be national, not federal," implying a greater role for the states.[55] More to the point, Bush informed the governors that he called the meeting to discuss national education policy "because you bear the constitutional responsibility for education."[56]

The emphasis was on downplaying the federal role in supplying federal aid. "Our focus must no longer be on our resources," Bush told the governors, but "must be on results."[57] His chief of staff, John Sununu, informed the gathering that the amount of money spent on a child's public schooling from federal, state and local coffers was sufficient and that "money . . . was therefore not the problem."[58] For Sununu, the problem was that with all the money spent on education, "the schools were not doing the job."[59] Consequently, the document that emerged from the summit—entitled the "Jefferson Compact"—stated that the "federal financial role is limited and has even declined" and that the only financial role left to the federal government was "to promote national education equity by helping our poor children" and "to provide research . . . for programs that work."[60]

The education summit established seven main goals. Three of those dealt with economic competitiveness: (1) setting training levels to "guarantee a competitive work force," (2) raising academic performances on international achievement tests and (3) developing a pool of qualified teachers and up-to-date technology.[61] Two other goals dealt with the old equity agenda: reducing illiteracy and the dropout rate. The other two goals were to have children prepared to start schooling and to create drug-free schools.

Bush structured his message to the governors by emphasizing outcomes. He rallied the governors to the "spirit of the summit," which was to answer the question, How can we get results?[62] He framed his plea with the statement that educational America "is still at risk" despite the fact that "our children are . . . the beneficiaries of a nation that lavishes unsurpassed resources on their schooling."[63]

To obtain educational results, Bush forwarded five main ideas for "tradition-shattering reform."[64] The most important of these, although mentioned third, was the concept of choice. The president foresaw the "day when choice among schools will be the norm rather than the exception—when parents will be full partners in the education of their children."[65] The other four were literacy, accountability (through testing), diversity and excellence.

Many observers felt that the education summit had, once again, placed a sharp national focus on education. The *New York Times* commented that "paying attention to the schools is a national mission now."[66] One Virginia newspaper commented that education, "the Democrats' issue," had been given a Republican context and that the Democrats may be "giving up part of their political birthright."[67]

Some educators concurred. Ernest L. Boyer, president of the Carnegie Corporation and former U.S. commissioner of education in the Carter administration, hailed the summit as "a breathtaking beginning of new affirmation of the work for the schools."[68] Dr. Scott Thompson, executive director of the National Association for Secondary Schools, gave President Bush high marks for his initiative.[69] AFT president Albert Shanker characterized Bush's speech at the summit as a "generous vision," partly because Bush had "failed to mention private schools"—a theme of the Reagan administration.[70]

There were critics. They grouped their arguments into four main issues; the lack of federal money for education, neglect of at-risk students, the advocacy of choice plans, and the lack of coherent national vision for education.

Money was a key. Dr. Thompson gave Bush even higher marks for his efforts should he "support specific programs with money."[71] Anne C. Lewis, educational columnist for *Phi Delta Kappan,* observed that money "was almost totally ignored at the Charlottesville summit."[72] Indeed, Boyer, who first suggested a summit, warned that without federal monies perhaps "he should scrap the whole thing."[73]

Some felt choice was a simplistic solution to a complex educational problem. "Choice is not a panacea," responded Gary Marx, associate director of the American Association of School Administrators; "it may upset the integration apple cart."[74]

Others feared that the rush to raise national standards would adversely affect at-risk students. Lester W. Young, Jr., assistant commissioner of education in New York, predicted that raising national standards "will create large numbers of students at risk."[75] Harold Howe II, Johnson's U.S. commissioner of education, underscored a faulty view of at-risk and poor students. He criticized the tunnel vision of policy makers who held to a narrow concept that "fixing schools will fix young people [and] nothing could be further from the reality [than the belief]."[76] What was needed beyond school reform, according to Howe, was a comprehensive social effort to help the poor.

Finally, President Bush was criticized for lacking a comprehensive national vision of education. Anne Lewis condemned the lack of a "semblance of true leadership . . . that can inspire people with a vision."[77] For Lewis, the Charlottesville conferees did not "say anything very important."[78] Educators now had the tools, she concluded, "but no blueprint on where to go from there."[79]

BUSH'S CHOICE PLAN

Bush's advocacy of choice for education was not a strong campaign issue; however, after the election, the president made choice the linchpin of his educational program. With strong presidential focus, choice became the major educational issue of the time, but it was not without its critics.

The choice concept was a simple one. Under choice, parents could send their children to any public school within a school system. This plan may have entailed sending students outside their district. The idea behind choice was that parents and students may gravitate to those schools they felt were best.

The choice concept had its origin in the 1960s during the battles for school integration in the cities. Urban school districts declared open enrollments in which students could attend schools of their preference. The aim of open enrollment was to have black (or white) students in a predominantly black (or white) school attend another school of their choice in order to integrate the schools best.

By the 1970s, choice had evolved into a program that proposed vouchers. The voucher plan was a more radical federal extension of choice. Under a voucher system, parents—with federal monies—could send their children to schools of their choice outside the public school system. They could choose private or parochial schools. The idea was first broached in this country in the 1960s by conservative economist Milton Friedman. The purpose of vouchers was to stimulate educational excellence through market competition. The best schools would attract the most students, and the ineffective schools would disappear.

The teacher unions adamantly opposed vouchers. They contended that vouchers would destroy public education. They pointed to Holland, where a largely public school system was transformed into a largely private system under a voucher plan. They argued that the public schools would be a repository of the poor and minorities in a two-tracked system.

Educational reformer Mario Fantini best devised a choice plan that would deflect the growing popularity of vouchers in conservative educational and political circles. In 1973, Fantini published his book, *Public Schools of Choice.*

Fantini's book was the first major effort to define a comprehensive choice plan. He had three main reasons for writing the book. First, Fantini believed that parents should have a greater say in the education of their children. (He had previously been a chief architect of the community control movement of the 1960s, demanding urban school boards elected by parents.) Second, he wanted a supermarket of ideas whereby the public schools would offer viable educational alternatives. Writing at the height of the "free school" and alternative school movement, Fantini felt that American education lacked sufficient variety. He noted that affluent families could choose a Montessori private school but that such an innovative approach was lacking in a public school. Third, Fantini opposed vouchers and wanted to deflect the growing movement toward vouchers. In the early 1970s, Christopher Jencks of Harvard persuaded the Office of Economic Opportunity to start a five-year voucher experiment in Alum Rock.

Fantini clearly denounced vouchers. He wrote:

To my mind, using education vouchers to make options outside the public school system—the external voucher plan—is far less important, far less desirable, than creating options within the system and making these available by choice, to parents, students and teachers...the public schools already have the capacity and the resources to operate such a system *internally*.[80]

Moreover, for Fantini the voucher plan had a hidden agenda as it was "undeniably skewed in the direction of nonpublic school options."[81] For Fantini, "The word 'public' in the Public Schools of Choice is crucial. The plan proposes a new framework for our *public* system of education."[82] For Fantini the key idea was alternative education, which he considered in his next book. However, Fantini sought to distinguish his public schools of choice from open enrollment plans; he was not entirely successful in clarifying the difference.

President Reagan had long been committed to the voucher plan. Moreover, he was extremely sympathetic to private and parochial schools. During his administration he proposed two different voucher plans. Both were successfully opposed by the two teacher unions, the National Education Association and the American Federation of Teachers AFL-CIO.

It followed, therefore, that Reagan would be enamored of choice. He called a White House Workshop on Choice ten days before leaving office in January 1989. The purpose was to give President-elect Bush a boost in his espousal of choice. Reagan termed choice "that marvelous program... that is fostering unprecedented competition among public schools to make them more attractive to parents and students."[83]

For Bush, choice was the new educational panacea. He argued that choice is "perhaps the single most promising of these ideas" in education.[84] Indeed, choice responded to a "simple but quite serious problem in education."[85] Bush linked choice to economic well-being, to a successful education that "is one of the surest paths out of poverty."[86]

Bush emphasized choice as mostly helping the poor. He argued that "it is the working poor and low-income families who suffer most from the absence of choice in the public schools."[87] He concluded that "for this reason alone...further expansion of public school choice is a national imperative."[88]

To promulgate choice nationwide, Secretary of Education Lauro F. Cavazos published a pamphlet arguing for choice, along with the statements of presidents Reagan and Bush, made at the White House conference, endorsing choice. In addition, Secretary Cavazos held numerous sessions throughout the nation discussing choice with educational leaders and the public.

The pamphlet enumerated eight reasons why states and localities should adopt choice plans. These reasons included the supposed ability of choice to develop individuality in students, foster competition, retain potential school dropouts, increase parents' input, help the poor educationally and restructure public schools. The most important reason, listed fourth, was that "choice can improve educational outcomes."[89] Choice, it was argued, was the necessary condition to improve educational achievement nationally.

With presidential focus, choice swept the educational scene. AFT president Albert Shanker called it "the hottest educational issue these days."[90] Chris Pipho of the Education Commission of the States exulted that "choice could become the darling of the new legislative ideas in 1989."[91] A 1987 Gallup Poll revealed that 71 percent of the polled American public endorsed choice—76 percent of public school parents and 81 percent of private and parochial school parents.[92] Two years later that support of the American public dwindled to 60 percent for, 31 percent against and 9 percent undecided.[93]

By 1989, some fifteen states were already considering choice. These included Arizona, Massachusetts, New York, California and Oklahoma.[94] The key choice plan was in Minnesota, which had adopted choice in the early 1980s. Choice watchers claimed that "everybody is waiting to see what happens in Minnesota."[95]

Let us summarize the arguments for and against choice. Proponents such as Fantini foresaw improvement in school achievement—the main policy outcome of education. Choice, they argued, would motivate teachers and administrators in a competitive environment. Moreover, such competition would create variety in education and the alternatives necessary to fine-tune our educational system. Most importantly, they reasoned, choice would reestablish the bedrock principle of democracy—participation. Parents and students would decide which schools the students would attend. For budget-minded policy makers, choice offered a no-cost solution to the complex problems of education in a technological society.

The opponents of choice were many and varied. They ranged from civil rights adherents to presidents of the nation's school boards to the largest teacher union, the National Education Association. The arguments marshaled against choice were as strong as those for it.

Critics argued that choice would not improve school achievement. As a no-cost solution, choice, they contended, could not reach the myriad educational problems without substantive programs and resources. Most importantly, they contended that choice would discriminate against the poor and minorities. Under such plans as that in Minnesota, they pointed out, parents had to pay for their own transportation to the schools of their choice—thus further burdening the poor who could not afford transportation.

They pointed out that problems of implementation were enormous. Teachers would lack input on decision making, and parents could not influence the school board in the districts in which they lived.

The teacher unions responded differently to choice. Although both unions had strongly opposed vouchers, they parted company on the concept of choice. Mary Hatwood Futrell, president of the NEA, found choice too problematic whereas AFT president Shanker, who had already supported the Fantini concept, muted his criticism.

Futrell perceived choice as but an entry to vouchers. After eight years of the Reagan-Bush administration's advocating vouchers, she was naturally suspicious. "Where we begin to be leery," she declared, "is when people start using choice as a euphemism for vouchers and tax credits."[96]

Moreover, she perceived choice as a negative solution. Her dislike was fundamentally philosophical. She contended that "education is not just another consumer item" but "the bedrock of our democracy" and that "quality education must be available in *every public school*."[97] She foresaw enormous organizational problems. She wondered what "will happen to the schools, students—and the school districts—left behind?"[98] Most importantly, she perceived choice as eroding parent power because departing parents would be unable to "influence school boards in districts where they do not live, vote or pay taxes."[99]

AFT president Shanker shared some of the NEA's fundamental philosophical uneasiness about choice. He wondered if the law of competition essential to the marketplace could be successfully transposed to education. Education was a public, not a private, sector responsibility, he argued. Business was motivated by the profit motive, whereas such a motive was absent in public schooling.

Still, Shanker perceived "many justifications for choice."[100] He warned that his misgivings did not constitute "an argument against choice."[101] He stated: "Parents and students would be more committed to a school if they chose it. Different kinds of schools are good for different kids, and choice makes better matches possible. Choice also could promote integration and attract private school students back into the public system."[102]

Nevertheless, he perceived choice to be limited in affecting school achievement. For Shanker, raising student achievement most probably will "come some other way."[103] He concluded that choice was primarily a political palliative for parents.

There were stronger critics of choice. An educational think tank, Designs for Change, conducted a damaging two-year study of choice programs in four large cities: New York, Chicago, Philadelphia and Boston.

The authors concluded that "choice presents so many dangers that it should not be pursued as a major strategy for educational improvement."[104] Their research of the program in the four cities revealed that students at risk were shunted aside in choice programs, "creating a new form of segregation based on a combination of race, income-level, and previous success at school."[105] They wrote:

In these school systems, school choice has, by and large, become a new improved method of student sorting, in which . . . black and hispanic students, low-income students, students with low achievement, students with absence and behavior problems, handicapped students, and limited English proficient students have very limited opportunities to participate in popular options [of] high schools and programs.[106]

According to the researchers, this sorting system for choosing the "best" students operated in a subtle manner. Students at risk or handicapped were not recruited for select high schools either because of lack of information or the persuasive powers of junior high school counselors. Too often these counselors attempted to build "their school's reputation by referring top-achieving students and discouraging 'risky' students."[107]

Moreover, the admissions process was a hurdle. The researchers found that "individual schools were able to exercise a great deal of discretion in deciding whom to admit."[108] In New York City, the majority of students were turned down—only 32,000 applicants received choice among 90,000 entering high school.[109]

Whatever the merits of choice, an American president, vaguely desiring to become an education president, once again set the national education agenda. It was another indication of the changing role of American presidents in education.

BUSH'S BULLY PULPIT

President-elect Bush's inaugural speech furnished lofty rhetoric on national goals but no mention of education. Instead, the new president invoked an upbeat mood. He proclaimed that "a new breeze is blowing" that would result in a "new activism."[110] The president noted that "we live in a peaceful, prosperous time" and that "the old solution" of federal money "could not solve the nation's problems."[111] The inaugural address intended to create an optimistic mood without providing specific programmatic plans.

However, President Bush's first major address to Congress after the inauguration was another matter. Bush submitted his budget, and he devoted a good share of his budget message to education. He announced:

The most important competitiveness program of all is one which improves education in America.

When some of our students actually have trouble locating America on the map of the world, it is time for us to map a new approach to education.

We must reward excellence, and cut through bureaucracy. We must help those schools that need help most. We must give choice to parents, students, teachers and principals. And we must hold all concerned accountable. In education, we cannot tolerate mediocrity.[112]

There were more specifics than inaugural rhetoric. Bush proposed to increase federal education spending while freezing the military defense budget. Bush asked for a $500 million program for five years to be given as a reward to those schools that merited it. He proposed a 20 percent increase in funds for the Head Start preschool program for poor children. He wanted to expand magnet schools, which would attract top students and faculty. He asked for a new program of National Science scholars. He admonished that some system of "alternate certification" be given to teachers who did not have training at schools of education but had valuable experience in business and other fields.

He concluded quite proudly that he had made good on his campaign promise: "I have said I'd like to be the Education President. Tonight I ask you to join me by becoming 'the Education Congress.' "[113]

In his first State of the Union message, Bush set specific national goals for excellence reform. The *New York Times* called these goals "the only major new aspect" dealing with domestic matters in the annual message.[114]

Bush targeted high aims for American education. His "ambitious program," he said, would "increase the high school graduation rate to no less than 90 percent."[115] Moreover, the president said that by the end of the century, "U.S. students must be first in math and science achievement in the world."[116] That achievement would also mean that "by the year 2000, every American adult must be... literate."[117] In order to be assured, such national goals would each have the president's proposed national testing in crucial subjects for students at the fourth, eighth and twelfth grades.

The president made clear that these ambitious national educational aims were crucial to the well-being of the American economy. "These investments," he declared, "will keep America competitive."[118] There was no alternative since "the future's at stake."[119] Consequently, he intoned that "the nation will not accept anything less than excellence in education."[120]

Critics of the State of the Union message reiterated familiar charges against the Bush program: lack of money and lack of a blueprint to achieve those goals. Despite increases in the Bush budget proposals for Head Start and literacy programs, congressional Democrats estimated the slight increase in the Bush budget was less than the inflation rate of 4.2 percent.[121] Again, educators such as Bill Honig, California's superintendent of schools and a supporter of excellence reform, felt that the president "has to commit the resources" to realize his educational goals.[122] Harold Howe II concluded that "a president should put his money where his mouth is."[123] However, supporters of excellence reform were satisfied with the bully pulpit approach and praised the president for making "education a national issue."[124]

Critics were puzzled how these "ambitious aims" could be achieved with large problems remaining in American education and American society. Poverty was mentioned. One educator concluded that the president's lack of a blueprint meant that the Bush proposal "with 20 percent of our kids living in poverty is ludicrous."[125]

The public did not view Bush as an education president. A *New York Times*-CBS poll indicated that fully 60 percent of the American public felt that regarding education, Bush had "mainly just talked about it."[126]

CONCLUSION

President Bush practiced a politics of educational minimalism. He resorted mainly to the bully pulpit to focus on education as a national issue while providing minimal federal funds. Nevertheless, he maintained the national interest in education set in motion by his predecessor. That interest was the offspring of a deteriorating economic position of the United States.

Still, it was the Bush White House that set the national agenda in education, and the president's strong advocacy of choice made it the dominant solution to the nation's educational problems.

NOTES

1. Anne C. Lewis, "Looking for Leadership," *Phi Delta Kappan,* June 1989, p. 748.

2. Ibid.

3. Edward B. Fiske, "How Education Came to Be a Campaign Issue," *New York Times,* January 3, 1988 (Education Supplement), Section 12, p. 32.

4. *Chronicle of Higher Education,* June 8, 1988, p. 1.

5. Fiske, "How Education Came to Be a Campaign Issue," p. 32.

6. Ibid.

7. Ibid.

8. Ibid., p. 34.

9. Ibid.

10. Interview with John Goodlad, Old Dominion University, Norfolk, Virginia, October 21, 1988.

11. *Chronicle of Higher Education,* November 2, 1988, p. 1.

12. George Kaplan, "New Beginnings, New Limits: Education and the 1988 Presidential Election," *Phi Delta Kappan,* October 1988, p. 122.

13. Fiske, "How Education Came to Be a Campaign Issue," p. 34.

14. *Chronicle of Higher Education,* November 2, 1988, p. A.18.

15. George Bush, "Statement of Vice-President Bush on Education" (Position Paper), Washington, D.C. 1988, p. 1.

16. Michael Dukakis, "On the Issues: Educational Opportunity for All" (Position Paper), Boston, Mass., 1988, p. 2.

17. Ibid., p. 1.

18. *New York Times,* July 22, 1988, p. A.10.

19. Ibid.

20. *New York Times,* August 19, 1988, p. A.14.

21. Ibid.

22. Ibid.

23. Ibid.

24. Ibid.

25. *Chronicle of Higher Education,* July 27, 1988, p. 14.

26. Ibid.

27. Ibid.

28. *Chronicle of Higher Education,* September 1, 1988, p. A.18.

29. Ibid.

30. *Chronicle of Higher Education,* October 5, 1988, p. 32.

31. *New York Times,* October 15, 1988, p. 11.

32. Ibid.

33. *New York Times,* February 10, 1989, p. A.17.

34. *New York Times,* September 11, 1988, p. E.30.

35. Ibid.

36. Ibid.

37. Ibid.

38. *New York Times,* September 11, 1988, p. A.32.

39. *Chronicle of Higher Education,* September 14, 1988, p. A.23.

40. Ibid., p. A.31.

41. Jeff Blyskal and Marie Hodge, "The Fault—and Default—in the STARS," *New York Times,* September 22, 1988, p. A.39.

42. Ibid.

43. George Bush (with Victor Gold), *Looking Forward* (New York: Doubleday, 1987), p. 25.

44. Ibid., p. 8.

45. Gail Sheehy, *Character: America's Search for Leadership* (New York: William Morrow, 1988), p. 156.

46. Bush, *Looking Forward,* p. 44.

47. Ibid.

48. Ibid.

49. Sheehy, *Character,* p. 160.

50. Ibid.

51. Albert Shanker, "Peak or Pique?" *New York Times,* September 17, 1989, p. E.7.

52. "Statement by the President and Governors," *New York Times,* October 1, 1989, Section 4, p. 22.

53. Anne C. Lewis, "A Box Full of Tools But No Blueprint," *Phi Delta Kappan,* November 1989, p. 180.

54. *New York Times,* September 27, 1989, p. B8.

55. George Bush, "Remarks by the President," The White House Office of the Press Secretary, Charlottesville, Va., September 28, 1989, p. 5.

56. Ibid.

57. Ibid.

58. Tom Wicker, "Bush's Report Card," *New York Times,* October 6, 1989, p. A31.

59. Ibid.

60. "Statement by the President and Governors," p. 22.

61. Ibid.

62. Bush, "Remarks by the President," p. 3.

63. Ibid., pp. 4-5.

64. Ibid., p. 6.

65. Ibid.

66. *New York Times,* October 1, 1989, Section 4, p. 1.

67. *Virginian Ledger-Star,* September 27, 1989, p. A.10.

68. *New York Times,* September 30, 1989, p. 9.

69. Ibid.

70. Albert Shanker, "A Generous Vision," *New York Times,* October 8, 1989, p. E.7.

71. *New York Times,* p. 9.

72. Lewis, "A Box Full of Tools But No Blueprint," p. 180.

73. Ibid.

74. *New York Times,* September 30, 1989, p. 9.

75. *New York Times,* December 6, 1989, p. 14.

76. Harold Howe II, "Letter to the Editor," *New York Times,* October 17, 1989, p. A.26.

77. Lewis, "A Box Full of Tools But No Blueprint," p. 180.

78. Ibid.

79. Ibid.

80. Mario D. Fantini, *Public Schools of Choice* (New York: Simon and Schuster, 1973), pp. 20-21.

81. Ibid., p. 20.

82. Ibid., p. 34.

83. Ronald Reagan, "Remarks on the White House Workshop on Choice in Education," *Improving Schools and Empowering Parents: Choice in American Education* (Washington, D.C.: U.S. Government Printing Office, October 1989), p. 29.

84. George Bush, "Remarks on the White House Workshop on Choice in Education," *Improving Schools and Empowering Parents: Choice in American Education* (Washington, D.C.: U.S. Government Printing Office, October 1989), p. 31.

85. Ibid.

86. Ibid., p. 32.

87. Ibid.

88. Ibid.

89. Ibid., p. 14.

90. Albert Shanker, "Competition and Choice: But Will Schools Improve?" *New York Times,* February 12, 1989, p. E.7.

91. Chris Pipho, "Switching Labels: From Vouchers to Choice," *Education Week,* February 1, 1989, p. 27.

92. Alec M. Gallup and David L. Clark, "The 19th Annual Gallup Poll of the Public's Attitudes Toward the Public Schools," *Phi Delta Kappan,* September 1987, p. 20.

93. Stanley E. Elam and Alec M. Gallup, "The 21st Annual Gallup Poll of the Public's Attitude Toward the Public Schools," *Phi Delta Kappan,* September 1989, p. 44.

94. Pipho, "Switching Labels," p. 27.

95. Ibid.

96. Mary Hatwood Futrell, "Real Parental Choice," *Education Week,* January 15, 1989, p. 12.

97. Ibid.

98. Ibid.

99. Ibid.

100. Shanker, "Competition and Choice," p. E.7.

101. Ibid.

102. Ibid.

103. Ibid.

104. Donald R. Moore and Suzanne Davenport, "School Choice: The New Improved Sorting Machine," National Invitational Conference on Public School Choice, Minneapolis, Minn., February 24, 1989, p. 1.

105. Ibid.

106. Ibid.

107. Ibid., p. 7.

108. Ibid.

109. Ibid.

110. George Bush, "Inaugural Address," *New York Times,* January 21, 1989, p. 10.

111. Ibid.

112. George Bush, "Address to Congress," *New York Times,* February 10, 1989, p. A.17.

113. Ibid.

114. *New York Times,* February 1, 1990, p. 1.

115. George Bush, "State of the Union Message," *New York Times,* February 1, 1990, p. D.22.

116. Ibid.

117. Ibid.

118. Ibid.

119. Ibid.

120. Ibid.

121. *New York Times,* February 2, 1990, p. A.19.

122. Ibid.

123. Harold Howe II to Maurice R. Berube, February 5, 1990.

124. *New York Times,* February 2, 1990, p. A.9.

125. Ibid.

126. *New York Times,* January 28, 1990, p. 25.

7

A National Framework

Questions remain concerning the role of the presidents in American education. Is there a need for some sort of national framework in education that would formalize a national concern in education? Since education is a state responsibility, is there need for a constitutional amendment to establish a national context for education?

It is quite clear that since World War II, a national policy in education has, in effect, existed. In his analysis of American education, revisionist historian Joel Spring concludes:

When all the major federal legislation and action in the areas of education since 1945 are studied, and the major educational changes on a national level are considered in terms of historical development, a coherent and clear national educational policy emerges. In other words, the sum total of historical events has created a national educational policy that exits but has not been *formally* stated (emphasis added).[1]

What is lacking, according to Spring, is a national educational policy that is "executed as a single, coherent plan."[2] Then, should a national government, with the president as a key actor, establish a formalized national framework of education that could help in setting a long-range national educational agenda?

A colleague and longtime educational reformer, Dwight Allen, has proposed such a national framework that deserves serious consideration and that may signal a large-scale discussion of the issue. In his new book, *Schools for a New Century,* Allen presents the educational establishment with a specific design for a national framework of education. Allen's prescription rests on the premise that American education is becoming more national in character. "The starting point for any rational, comprehensive reform of the American schools," he wrote, "has to be the establishment of some sort of national framework."[3]

Allen's National School Board would exercise a wide range of powers. The board would develop standards for certification, create experimental schools and establish a national curriculum. With regard to curriculum, Allen would have the national board determine two-thirds of the curriculum and the states and localities determine the remaining third. Moreover, school finance would be a federal responsibility.

Allen's proposals would not only revolutionize education in America but, perhaps, shift the seat of influence. An independent National School Board in the Supreme Court model may remove the president and Congress as the educational shapers they have been since World War II. In that respect, Allen is in tune with American voters who want national direction but who are fearful of a formalized role of the president and Congress. In a 1989 Gallup Poll, only 5 percent of the American public were in favor of a presidential and congressional influence establishing national achievement standards and goals. Fully 61 percent were in favor of leaving such a task to professional educators.[4]

Allen's supreme court in education would probably limit the president's role to the appointment of National School Board members, as is the case with the Supreme Court. But, as in the Supreme Court, appointments would become intensely political, with presidential appointees reflecting, for the most part, both the political and educational philosophy of a political party.

There already has been increased politicization of education; however, a final national framework could seriously intensify the political process in education. For Dr. Madeline Hunter, a pioneer in teaching methodology, such a politicization of education could bring about a "serendipitous dividend": the intense national political debate in education may result in Americans' "becoming literate about education."[5] Hunter bemoans the American public's lack of awareness of the complexity of teaching and the considerable research body on teaching methodology since the 1960s.

One political problem with a coherent national educational policy is whose policy it may be. There has been a sharp divergence in national education policy in the past generation between the two political parties. The Democratic party, comprised of many blacks and other minorities, has continued its advocacy of educational issues of the equity agenda: poverty and at-risk students. The Republican party, for the most part, has banked its fortunes on the excellence agenda: helping the best students reverse America's economic decline.

One example of potential controversy would center on which political party's curriculum one would adopt. William Bennett's curriculum for his model James Madison Elementary School and James Madison High School is a case in point. Bennett's suggested reading in literature at these schools almost wholly neglects authors who are not white, male and/or American or European. This curriculum has been the subject of intense criticism.

Every major industrialized nation has a national system of education—communist countries as well as democratic countries. These countries have national ministries of education that often determine the relationship between education and the economy. Only the United States among major industrialized nations persists in a vague, decentralized and informal system. Nevertheless, there are signs that the American public—and official policy makers—is emerging from a severe cultural lag in education.

A case in point is the Japanese educational system, which is typical of industrialized nations. Its focal point is the Ministry of Education, which operates as the leading policy-making body with two other bodies on a prefectural and municipal level. The Ministry of Education has considerable power over the system. Specific responsibilities include determining curriculum standards and textbooks, supervising higher education and regulating private schools. Moreover, the national government provides nearly half of the total education budget in Japan.

The lower bodies have less control over education. On a prefectural level, the key responsibilities involve the board of education's appointing a superintendent and licensing teachers. On a municipal level, the local board oversees the day-to-day operation of the schools and refers other matters to higher educational authorities.

The prime minister of Japan wields considerable power. He appoints the minister of education and, with cabinet approval, all the members of the Central Council for Education, which is the educational unit that establishes broad education policy, which the Ministry of Education implements.[6]

THE CONSTITUTIONAL QUESTION

Proceeding with this thinking, one wonders whether a constitutional amendment may be necessary to establish a national framework of education. Under Article X of the U.S. Constitution all powers not specifically mentioned "are reserved to the States respectively."[7] Moreover, the U.S. Supreme Court in the 1974 *Rodriguez* decision on school finance reiterated that education was not a right under our Constitution.

First, let us examine whether the individual states, following the reasoning of Article X and the *Rodriguez* decision, either declared in their respective constitutions that education was a right or made education an important part of their state functions.

Only three states have declared education a fundamental right in their constitutions. Each state provides a section at the beginning of its constitution to enumerate a declaration of rights; nearly all of these declarations resemble the U.S. Constitution's Bill of Rights. For example, commonly declared as rights are due process, religious freedom, habeas corpus, bail, trial by jury and the right to private property. Only North Carolina, Wyoming and Ohio list education as a separate right.

The most emphatic declaration of the right to education is in North Carolina's constitution. Still, the language is somewhat confusing, defining education as both a right and a privilege. The constitution reads: "The people have a right to the privilege of education, and it is the duty of the state to guard and maintain that right.[8]"

Wyoming's declaration follows suit. That constitution declares that "the right of the citizen to opportunities should have practical recognition."[9] Consequently, it instructs the legislature to "suitably encourage means and agencies" that will "advance the sciences and liberal arts."[10]

The Ohio Constitution lumps the right to education with religious and moral rights. It directs the General Assembly "to encourage schools as the means of instruction."[11] None of the other forty-seven state constitutions mentions education in the section declaring rights.

Moreover, under state functions four state constitutions fail to devote a separate section to education. In the Pennsylvania, Tennessee, Vermont and Minnesota constitutions, education is subsumed under other headings. However, all of the state constitutions provide for the establishment of public school systems and public higher education systems, but the treatments vary in length and detail.

There is no correlation between the length of the educational portion of the state constitution and state support of education. For example, Pennsylvania's constitution is the shortest on education and totals five lines, mainly establishing a public school system "to serve the needs of the commonwealth."[12] By contrast, Mississippi devotes nearly half a dozen pages outlining educational responsibilities. Both in financial level of support and in academic quality there should be little to dispute Pennsylvania's supremacy over Mississippi in education.

Moreover, there is considerable variation in the type of educational duty prescribed. Some state constitutions, such as those of Arkansas and Illinois, detail funding procedures. Western states such as Idaho, Montana and Oregon link the sale of public lands to education. Some such as Louisiana and California outline methods of selecting school boards and university trustees, and California goes furthest by mentioning desired teacher salary levels and procedures to select textbooks. Most forbid the use of state funds for religious schools.

There is no standard format. Georgia's constitution provides for educational assistance. A portion is devoted to establishing "grants, scholarships, loans, or other assistance to students and parents."[13] On the other hand, the Massachusetts Constitution retains its colonial language. It specifies the creation of Harvard College, 1636, a private college today, "by our wise and pious ancestors . . . in which university many persons of great eminence have, by the blessing of GOD, been initiated in the arts and sciences, which qualified them for public employments, both in Church and State."[14]

A standard format has been suggested by the group that publishes the constitutions. The Columbia University panel that regularly prints updated versions proposes a minimalist model state constitution. The group, the Legislative Drafting Research Fund, calls for the legislature to "provide for the maintenance and support of a system of free public schools open to all children in the state ... including public institutions of higher learning."[15] Comprising but fifty-two words, the model constitution omits detailed specification of educational functions. Most importantly, it fails to include education as a right.

In summary, the state constitutions, for the most part, do not declare that education is a right. Moreover, the variation of educational duties in these constitutions does not match the degree to which a state is involved in education.

PRESIDENTIAL PRECEDENCE

There has been some precedence for presidents' seeking a constitutional amendment for education. Both Thomas Jefferson and Ulysses Grant sought constitutional amendments for a national system of education, and, in recent times, Ronald Reagan sought a constitutional amendment to restore school prayer to the schools.

Jefferson perceived the importance of education to the nation. Consequently, in his sixth annual message to Congress in 1806, he called for a constitutional amendment in education. His idea was for a national system that would cooperate with the states. Moreover, he proposed using federal monies from the sale of public lands to finance this new national system. The latter recommendation prompted some advocates of a constitutional amendment, much later, to feel that perhaps Jefferson "went too far."[16]

Jefferson used the occasion of a federal budget surplus to make his plea for a constitutional amendment. He emphatically told Congress:

Education is here placed among the articles of public care.... A public institution can alone supply these sciences, though rarely called for, are yet necessary to complete the circle, all the parts of which contribute to the improvement of the country and some of them to its preservation....

I suppose an amendment to the constitution ... [for] ... the present consideration of a national establishment for education.[17]

The idea took root. In 1875, President Ulysses S. Grant proposed in his State of the Union message that "a constitutional amendment be submitted to the Legislatures of the several states" in order to make "it the duty of each of the states to establish and forever maintain free public schools."[18] However, the Grant proposal refrained from mentioning federal funding.

The idea was maintained until the end of the nineteenth century. John C. Henderson, a Jeffersonian scholar, endorsed the concept as late as 1890. "Let a wisely worded provision be incorporated into the Constitution of the United States," he wrote, "making it the specific duty of the national government to duly cherish the interests of learning in all the states and territories beneath the American flag."[19]

The idea of a constitutional amendment in education has modern-day currency. In 1982, President Ronald Reagan introduced a constitutional amendment in Congress to permit prayer in the public schools. Although this amendment departed from establishing a national system of education, it was in that tradition. Moreover, the Reagan attempt was instructive for examining the politics of constitutional amendments with large-scale public suport.

The Reagan amendment was defeated in the Senate. Introduced by ultra-conservative senator Jesse Helms (R–N.C.), the constitutional amendment was subjected to a lengthy filibuster by Senate liberals. The liberals prevailed, and the constitutional amendment was defeated by a vote of fifty-three to forty-five.[20] One fallout of the debate was to create a strong sentiment against a constitutional amendment. Eight years later, President Bush's desire for a constitutional amendment to overturn a Supreme Court decision that would allow citizens to burn American flags in protest was rejected by members of Congress. There was widespread feeling after these attempts that constitutional amendments should be resorted to sparingly.

The school prayer issue was the result of a 1962 Supreme Court decision that prayer in public schools violated the Constitution in maintaining a separation of church and state. In the school prayer ruling conservatives found an issue that seemed to strike a symbolic nerve. For them the loss of prayer in the schools was but another step in the decline of discipline in the public schools, of morality in the larger society and of the work ethic. Restoration of school prayer in the public schools was perceived as the first step to restoring America. School prayer became a priority of the emerging new right, and Ronald Reagan made it a campaign pledge in 1980.

Indeed, public opinion polls seemed to indicate that the American public wanted to have a constitutional amendment to restore school prayer to the public schools. In 1974, for example, a large majority sampled in a Gallup Poll—77 percent of respondents—were in favor of such an amendment.[21] (They were also in favor of three other constitutional amendments in education: to authorize federal aid to parochial schools, to forbid busing for school integration and to equalize monies among schools.) Indeed, one Catholic lay journal, *Commonweal,* opposed to school prayer, conceded that "the 1962 Supreme Court ruling has never sat well with a large proportion of the American public."[22]

Moreover, even after the defeat of the Reagan gambit, the public still desired a constitutional amendment. In 1984, a follow-up Gallup Poll question revealed that 69 percent of the American public still desired a constitutional amendment to permit school prayer in the public schools.[23]

The key to President Reagan's proposal was to make school prayer voluntary. The proposed constitutional amendment read: "Nothing in this Constitution shall be construed to prohibit individual or group prayer in schools or other public institutions. No person shall be required by the United States or by any State to participate in prayer.[24]

In May 1982, Reagan announced his support of the amendment to a selective group of religious leaders and members of Congress. He declared that "prayer is still a powerful force in America."[25] He lamented the "current interpretation of our Constitution [that] holds that the minds of our children cannot be free to pray to God in the public schools."[26] Therefore, the president declared his resolve to "submit to the United States Congress a proposal to amend our Constitution to allow our children to pray in school."[27] He hoped that "the amendment we'll propose will restore the right to pray."[28]

Why did the Reagan proposal fail? The support was soft; very little political mobilization was mustered by proponents. One Rhode Island state legislator typified public response by declaring that he did not care deeply "if we do or don't have a prayer at the beginning of the school day."[29]

On the other hand, the opposition was both vocal and organized. A broad spectrum of moderate religious groups, liberals and civil libertarians maintained a steady drumbeat of opposition. Most importantly, the two teacher unions—the National Education Association and the American Federation of Teachers, AFL-CIO—used their considerable political muscle to derail the Reagan attempt.

Despite the support of the evangelical wing of American Christianity, the liberal religious sector objected vociferously to the Reagan amendment. In the liberal, intellectual Protestant journal, *The Christian Century*, editor James M. Wall perceived the "voluntary" character as being "designed to get around the obvious problem" of a violation of the separation of church and state.[30] Still, Wall considered the amendment "an implied pressure on the non-participating child, especially in a school predominantly of one faith."[31] However, Wall was aware that the Reagan amendment would "enhance the president's image with the conservative religious constituency which helped him gain the White House."[32]

Liberal Catholic journals also voiced discontent over the proposed amendment. *Commonweal*, a Catholic intellectual journal edited by the laity, concluded that "public school prayer is not the solution" that the religious right believes it to be.[33] The editorialist argued that "those prayers will be doctrinally specific, and offensive to those strong beliefs."[34] *America*, edited by American Jesuits, contended that "it is extremely unlikely that [school prayer] . . . is apt to make any significant contribution to the religious life of the children of our country."[35]

Moreover, some black clergy also dissented. The Rev. M. William Howard, executive director of the Black Council of the Reformed Church in America, added his objections to the amendment. He characterized the Reagan proposal as a "bold and unacceptable interference by the state in religious devotion."[36] He adopted the civil libertarian's credo that American democracy consists of "the respect we have for the rights of others to believe and to teach their children as they choose."[37]

Finally, AFT president Albert Shanker typified the response from educators. He concluded that the Supreme Court decision "made a lot of sense."[38] He related an incident in seventh grade in which religious bigotry subjected him to beatings by school bullies. His teacher had unintentionally triggered the violence by remarking that Shanker need not sing Christmas carols since he was Jewish and "doesn't believe in God."[39] The result was that Shanker was subjected to "frequent beatings by other students outside of school because of her remark."[40]

WHAT EXPERTS THINK

What do scholarly experts think about a constitutional amendment? Twenty national experts in educational policy responded to a purposeful sample mailed by the author. A purposeful sample is a nonrandomized sample of a subgroup—such as experts in a field—that may give highly useful qualitative data. A majority opposed a constitutional amendment that would establish the right to education. Eleven were opposed, seven were in favor, two believed it already implicit in the Constitution, and one was undecided.

One widely published author on the politics of education, Frederick Wirt of the University of Illinois, challenged the appropriateness of the question. "The question raised [of a constitutional amendment]," Wirt wrote, "has never been addressed in any scholarly or political discussions I have experienced."[41]

On the other hand, two respondents who were in leading policy roles in the Reagan and Johnson administrations did not view the question of a constitutional amendment as irrelevant. Former secretary of education Terrel Bell, who sparked the excellence reform movement with *A Nation at Risk,* thought that such a constitutional amendment was necessary.[42] The former U.S. commissioner of education in the Johnson administration, Harold Howe II, believed that such powers were already implicit in the Constitution and that "other cases [besides the *Rodriguez* decision] should be brought to test this issue in the Supreme Court."[43]

A minority of scholars of educational policy agreed with Bell. David Kratwohl of Syracuse University believed that there should be a constitutional amendment and wondered about "alternative guarantees" since he felt that in the absence of an amendment "there obviously should be some guarantees, possibly in the state constitutions."[44] David Kapel, editor of the *Urban Review,* perceived education "as a fundamental right as it allows individuals to move up the social scale."[45] The radical educational sociologist Stanley Aronowitz of City University was hesitant to endorse a constitutional amendment "to solve all of the nation's problems regarding racism, sexism and other forms of discrimination."[46] Nevertheless, Aronowitz favored an amendment for education because "education has become a fundamental right in an economic, political and social environment."[47] Dwight Allen favored "a constitutional amendment only if it is politically expedient."[48]

One professor who endorsed the Howe view was Howe's colleague at Harvard, Charles Vert Willie. A black scholar, Willie reflected the view of other black scholars by contending that the right to education is implicit under the Fourteenth Amendment of the Constitution. Willie declared that "the issue is not whether education is a right" but "whether the various levels of government . . . will enforce the Constitution's requirements in existence regarding the Fourteenth Amendment."[49]

Two key advocates of excellence reform opposed an amendment. Chester E. Finn, Jr., former assistant secretary of education in the Reagan administration, and his coauthor on some excellence reports, Diane Ravitch of Columbia University, were not in favor of such an amendment. Finn held that education was a "proper function of the states."[50] Ravitch feared "messing with the constitution" since, in her view, "amendments should be rare."[51]

A wide political range of scholars—liberal, conservative, radical—were not in favor of an amendment. Some like neo-conservative Harvard professor Nathan Glazer repeated Ravitch's reasoning that "we have enough constitutional amendments and we open the way to unnecessary litigation."[52] Allan Odden of the University of Southern California agreed that education was "important" but "not enough so as to change the constitution."[53] Gerald Grant of Syracuse University concurred, feeling that such an amendment "was unnecessary at this time."[54]

Other radical scholars opposed an amendment from a different vantage point. Political scientist Marilyn Gittell of City University and historian Joel Spring of the University of Cincinnati did not perceive a need for an amendment. Spring wrote that he did not "believe that educational policies should be linked to other national policies," a tendency that he perceived to be the case since World War II.[55]

CONCLUSION

What are we to conclude? First, we have seen that presidential leadership in education has increased since World War II, much of it determined by the economic needs of the nation. Roosevelt and Truman were concerned with a work force returning from the war that had to cope with a more sophisticated economy. Kennedy and Johnson sought a more economic well-being of American society by helping the poor educationally. These policies of educating the disadvantaged were continued by Nixon, Ford and Carter. Reagan, followed by Bush, responded to a more acute economic condition—the deterioration of the American economy from intense foreign competition. Only Eisenhower concentrated on a noneconomic threat—the space race with the Soviet Union and heating up the cold war.

Second, in the past generation there has been a growing awareness by the American public and policy makers of the vital importance of education to economic prosperity. Opinion polls have indicated the public's desire for national leadership in education for America successfully to compete economically.

Third, presidential candidates and cabinet aides have perceived the need for some presidential direction in education, no matter how vague. Secretary of Education Terrel Bell concluded that the nation "should be galvanized into a nationwide program."[56] In 1988 George Bush declared himself an education president. Democratic presidential candidate Michael Dukakis echoed similar sentiments by declaring that the president of the United States becomes this nation's number one advocate for education. It did not matter that these advocates for presidential leadership had no clear idea of the role of the president in education; they perceived the need to rethink that role.

Fourth, the role of the president still is confined by constitutional constraints. Whether the future reassessment of education and the presidency will result in a constitutional amendment or a continuation of the rhetorical presidency with the president as "teacher and preacher-in-chief" remains to be seen. Surely, the implications of the excellence reform movement suggest a greater role for the president and federal leadership.

Finally, education in the nation responds to socioeconomic and political realities beyond the confines of the schoolhouse door. This fact has meant that government, especially the federal government, will be perceived by the public as the educational leader and will continue to assume that function. The final arbiter of national educational policy may continue to be the president of the United States.

NOTES

1. Joel Spring, *The Sorting Machine Revisited: National Educational Policy Since 1945* (New York: Longman, 1989), pp. 172-73.

2. Ibid., p. 17.

3. Dwight Allen, *Schools for a New Century* (New York: Praeger, 1990), p. 30.

4. Stanley E. Elam and Alec M. Gallup, "The 21st Annual Gallup Poll of the

Public's Attitudes Toward the Public Schools," *Phi Delta Kappan,* September 1989, p. 44.

5. Dwight Allen (with Maurice R. Berube and Madeline Hunter), "Local Control and National Goals," Teleconference, Old Dominion University, Norfolk, Va., January 16, 1990.

6. U.S. Department of Education, *Japanese Education Today* (Washington, D.C.: U.S. Government Printing Office, 1989), p. 7.

7. *Constitutions of the United States: United States Constitution* (Dobbs Ferry, N.Y.: Oceana Publications, 1989), p. 12.

8. *Constitutions of the United States: North Carolina* (Dobbs Ferry, N.Y.: Oceana Publications, 1989), p. 2.

9. *Constitutions of the United States: Wyoming* (Dobbs Ferry, N.Y.: Oceana Publications, 1989), p. 3.

10. Ibid.

11. *Constitutions of the United States: Ohio* (Dobbs Ferry, N.Y.: Oceana Publications, 1988), p. 2.

12. *Constitutions of the United States: Pennsylvania* (Dobbs Ferry, N.Y.: Oceana Publications, 1987), p. 8.

13. *Constitutions of the United States: Georgia* (Dobbs Ferry, N.Y.: Oceana Publications, 1986), p. 39.

14. *Constitutions of the United States: Massachusetts* (Dobbs Ferry, N.Y.: Oceana Publications, 1985), p. 28.

15. *Constitutions of the United States: A Model State Constitution* (Dobbs Ferry, N.Y.: Oceana Publcations, 1989), p. 18.

16. John C. Henderson, *Thomas Jefferson's Views on Education* (New York: AMS Press, 1970, reprinted from the 1980 edition), p. 353.

17. Thomas Jefferson, *The Writings of Thomas Jefferson,* vol. 8 (Washington, D.C.: Taylor and Maury, 1856), pp. 68-69.

18. Henderson, *Thomas Jefferson's Views on Education,* p. 373.

19. Ibid., p. 379.

20. *Phi Delta Kappan,* December 1982, p. 292.

21. George C. Gallup, "Sixth Annual Gallup Poll of the Public's Attitude Toward Public Schools," *Phi Delta Kappan,* September 1974, p. 25.

22. *Commonweal,* May 21, 1982, p. 291.

23. George C. Gallup, "Sixteenth Annual Gallup Poll of the Public's Attitude Toward Public Schools," *Phi Delta Kappan,* September 1984, p. 35.

24. Ronald Reagan, "School Prayer Amendment," *American Education,* July 1982, p. 13.

25. Ibid., p. 12.

26. Ibid., p. 13.

27. Ibid.

28. Ibid.

29. David R. Carlins, Jr., "Trivality and the Prayer Amendment," *The Christian Century,* July 21-28, 1982, p. 782.

30. James M. Wall, "A Troubled Nation May Consider Prayer," *The Christian Century,* June 2, 1982, p. 651.

31. Ibid.

32. Ibid.

33. *Comonweal,* May 21, 1982, p. 292.

34. Ibid.

35. *America,* May 22, 1982, p. 391.

36. M. William Howard, "How the School Prayer Amendment Attacks Religious Liberty," *Education Digest,* December 1982, p. 13.

37. Ibid.

38. Albert Shanker, "Nothing 'Voluntary' in School Prayer," *New York Times,* November 9, 1982, p. E.9.

39. Ibid.

40. Ibid.

41. Frederick Wirt to Maurice R. Berube, January 30, 1990.

42. Terrel Bell to Maurice R. Berube, January 29, 1990.

43. Harold Howe II to Maurice R. Berube, January 23, 1990.

44. David Kratwohl to Maurice R. Berube, January 29, 1990.

45. David Kapel to Maurice R. Berube, January 30, 1990.

46. Stanley Aronowitz to Maurice R. Berube, March 9, 1990.

47. Ibid.

48. Dwight Allen to Maurice R. Berube, January 24, 1990.

49. Charles Vert Willie to Maurice R. Berube, January 24, 1990.

50. Chester E. Finn, Jr., to Maurice R. Berube, January 30, 1990.

51. Diane Ravitch to Maurice R. Berube, February 7, 1990.

52. Nathan Glazer to Maurice R. Berube, January 24, 1990.

53. Allan Odden to Maurice R. Berube, January 24, 1990.

54. Gerald Grant to Maurice R. Berube, January 29, 1990.

55. Joel Spring to Maurice R. Berube, February 7, 1990.

56. Terrel H. Bell, *The Thirteenth Man: A Reagan Cabinet Memoir* (New York: Free Press, 1988), p. 163.

Bibliography

Allen, Dwight. *Schools for a New Century*. New York: Praeger, forthcoming.
———— (with Maurice R. Berube and Madeline Hunter). "Local Control and National Goals." Teleconference. Old Dominion University, Norfolk, Va., January 16, 1990.
Ambrose, Stephen E. *Eisenhower: The President*. Vol. 2. New York: Simon and Schuster, 1983.
————. *Nixon: The Education of a Politician, 1913-1962*. New York: Simon and Schuster, 1987.
The American Assembly. *Goals for Americans*. New York: Prentice-Hall, 1960.
Annals of Congress. 14th Congress 2d Session, 1817. Washington, D.C.: U.S. Government Printing Office, 1817.
Ashline, Nelson F., Thomas R. Pezzullo, and Charles I. Norris, eds. *Education, Inequality and National Policy*. Lexington, Mass.: Lexington Books, 1976.
Banfield, Edward. *The Unheavenly City*. Boston: Little, Brown, 1970.
Basker, Roy, ed. *The Collected Works of Abraham Lincoln. Vol. VII, 1863-1864*. New Brunswick, N.J.: Rutgers University Press, 1953.
Bell, Daniel. *The Coming of Post-Industrial Society*. New York: Basic Books, 1973.
Bell, Terrel H. *The Thirteenth Man: A Reagan Cabinet Memoir*. New York: Free Press, 1988.
Bennett, William J. *James Madison High School*. Washington, D.C.: U.S. Department of Education, 1987.
————. *American Education: Making It Work*. Washington, D.C.: U.S. Department of Education, 1988.
————. *James Madison Elementary School*. Washington, D.C.: U.S. Department of Education, 1988.
————. *Our Children and Our Country: Improving America's Schools and Affirming the Common Culture*. New York: Simon and Schuster, 1988.
Berube, Maurice R. "Education and the Poor." *Commonweal*, March 31, 1967.
————. "Head Start to Nowhere." *Commonweal*, May 30, 1969.

————. *The Urban University in America.* Westport, Conn.: Greenwood Press, 1978.

————. *Education and Poverty: Effective Schooling in the United States and Cuba.* Westport, Conn.: Greenwood Press, 1984.

————. *Teacher Politics: The Influence of Unions.* Westport, Conn.: Greenwood Press, 1988.

Blyskal, Jeff, and Marie Hodge. "The Fault—and DeFault—in the STARS." *New York Times,* September 22, 1988.

Book Review Digest. New York: R.R. Bowker, 1963.

Bragdon, Henry Wilkinson. *Woodrow Wilson: The Academic Years.* Cambridge, Mass.: Harvard University Press, 1967.

Bullock, Henry Allen. *A History of Negro Education in the South: From 1616 to the Present.* Cambridge, Mass.: Harvard University Press, 1967.

Burk, Robert F. *Dwight D. Eisenhower: Hero and Politician.* Boston: Twayne, 1986.

Burner, David. *Herbert Hoover: A Public Life.* New York: Knopf, 1979.

Burns, James MacGregor. *John F. Kennedy: A Political Profile.* New York: Harcourt, Brace, 1959.

Bush, George. "Statement of Vice-President Bush on Education." Position Paper. Washington, D.C., 1988.

————. "Inaugural Address." *New York Times,* January 21, 1989.

————. "Address to Congress." *New York Times,* February 10, 1989.

————. "Remarks by the President." The White House Office of the Press Secretary, Charlottesville, Va., September 28, 1989.

————. "Remarks on the White House Workshop on Choice in Education." *Improving Schools and Empowering Parents: Choice in American Education.* Washington, D.C.: U.S. Government Printing Office, October 1989.

————. "State of the Union Message." *New York Times,* February 1, 1990.

———— (with Victor Gold). *Looking Forward.* New York: Doubleday, 1987.

Caldwell, Robert Granville. *James A. Garfield: Party Chieftain.* Hamden, Conn.: Archon Books, 1965.

Califano, Joseph A., Jr. *Governing America.* New York: Simon and Schuster, 1981.

Carlins, David R., Jr. "Triviality and the Prayer Amendment." *The Christian Century,* July 21-28, 1982.

Caro, Robert. *The Path to Power: The Early Years of Lyndon Johnson.* New York: Knopf, 1982.

Carter, Jimmy. *Why Not the Best?* Nashville, Tenn.: Broad Press, 1975.

————. "State of the Union Message." *New York Times,* January 20, 1978.

————. *Keeping Faith: Memoirs of a President.* New York: Bantam Books, 1982.

Cater, Douglass. "Oral History Interview." Austin, Tex.: Lyndon B. Johnson Presidential Library, April 29, 1969.

Chafe, William H. *The Unfinished Journey: America Since World War II.* New York: Oxford University Press, 1986.

Chavez, Jose. "Presidential Influence on the Politics of Higher Education: The Higher Education Act of 1965." Ann Arbor, Mich.: University Microfibus, 1975.

Clowse, Barbara Barksdale. *Brainpower for the Cold War: The Sputnik Crisis and the National Defense Education Act of 1958.* Westport, Conn.: Greenwood Press, 1981.

Cohen, Wilbur. "Oral History Interview." Austin, Tex.: Lyndon B. Johnson Presidential Library, March 2, 1969.

Commins, Saxe, ed. *Basic Writings of George Washington.* New York: Random House, 1948.

Congressional Record. 85th Congress, 2d Session, 1958. Washington, D.C.: U.S. Government Printing Office, 1958.

———. 89th Congress, 1st Session, 1965. Washington, D.C.: U.S. Governing Printing Office, 1965.

Constitutions of the United States: A Model State Constitution. Dobbs Ferry, N.Y.: Oceana Publications, 1989.

Constitutions of the United States: Georgia. Dobbs Ferry, N.Y.: Oceana Publications, 1986.

Constitutions of the United States: Massachusetts. Dobbs Ferry, N.Y.: Oceana Publications, 1985.

Constitutions of the United States: North Carolina. Dobbs Ferry, N.Y.: Oceana Publications, 1989.

Constitutions of the United States: Ohio. Dobbs Ferry, N.Y.: Oceana Publications, 1988.

Constitutions of the United States: Pennsylvania. Dobbs Ferry, N.Y.: Oceana Publications, 1987.

Constitutions of the United States: United States Constitution. Dobbs Ferry, N.Y.: Oceana Publications, 1989.

Constitutions of the United States: Wyoming. Dobbs Ferry, N.Y.: Oceana Publications, 1989.

Cremin, Lawrence A. *American Education: The National Experience 1783-1876.* New York: Harper and Row, 1980.

Daily Diary of President Lyndon B. Johnson. Frederick, Md.: University Publications of America, 1980.

Dukakis, Michael. "On the Issues: Educational Opportunity for All." Position Paper. Boston, Mass., 1988.

The Economic Reports of the President: January, 1948, January, 1947, July, 1947. New York: Reynal and Hitchcock, 1948.

The Economic Reports of the President: 1950-1952. Washington, D.C.: U.S. Government Printing Office, 1952.

Economic Report of the President 1990. Washington, D.C.: U.S. Government Printing Office, 1990.

Eddy, Edward Danforth, Jr. *Colleges for Our Land and Time: The Land-Grant Idea in American Education.* New York: Harper and Brothers, 1957.

Eisenhower, Dwight D. "Press Conference." *New York Times,* October 31, 1957.

———. "Education Message to Congress." *New York Times,* January 28, 1958.

———. *Waging Peace.* Garden City, N.Y.: Doubleday, 1965.

Elam, Stanley E., and Alec M. Gallup. "The 21st Annual Gallup Poll of the Public's Attitudes Toward the Public Schools." *Phi Delta Kappan,* September 1989.

Elmore, Richard F., and Milbrey Wallin McLaughlin. *Reform and Retrenchment: The Politics of California School Finance Reform.* Cambridge, Mass.: Ballinger, 1982.

Fantini, Mario D. *Public Schools of Choice.* New York: Simon and Schuster, 1973.

Field, L.H. Butler, ed. *Letters of Benjamin Rush*. Vol. 1. Princeton, N.J.: Princeton University Press, 1951.

Finn, Chester E., Jr. *Education and the Presidency*. Lexington, Mass.: Lexington Books, 1977.

————. "What Ails Education Research?" *Educational Research*, January-February, 1988.

Fiske, Edward B. "How Education Came to Be a Campaign Issue." *New York Times* (Education Supplement), January 3, 1988.

Foner, Philip S., ed. *Basic Writings of Thomas Jefferson*. Garden City, N.Y.: Halcyon House, 1944.

Ford, Gerald R. "My Vision of Education." *American Education*, April 1976.

————. *A Time to Heal*. New York: Harper and Row, 1979.

Friedman, Benjamin M. *Day of Reckoning: The Consequence of American Economic Policy Under Reagan and After*. New York: Random House, 1988.

Futrell, Mary Hatwood. "Real Parental Choice." *Education Week*, January 15, 1989.

Galbraith, John Kenneth. *The Affluent Society*. Boston: Houghton Mifflin, 1958.

————. *The New Industrial State*. Boston: Houghton Mifflin, 1967.

Gallup, Alec M. "The 13th Annual Gallup Poll of the Public's Attitudes Toward the Public Schools." *Phi Delta Kappan*, September 1981.

Gallup, Alec M., and David L. Clark. "The 19th Annual Gallup Poll of the Public's Attitudes Toward the Public Schools," *Phi Delta Kappan*, September 1987.

Gallup, Alec M. and Stanley E. Elam. "The 20th Annual Gallup Poll of the Public's Attitudes Toward the Public Schools." *Phi Delta Kappan*, September 1988.

Gallup, George C. "Sixth Annual Poll of the Public's Attitudes Toward Public Schools." *Phi Delta Kappan*, September 1974.

————. "Sixteenth Annual Gallup Poll of the Public's Attitudes Toward Public Schools." *Phi Delta Kappan*, September 1984.

Garrow, David J. *Bearing the Cross: Martin Luther King, Jr., and the Southern Christian Leadership Conference*. New York: Morrow, 1986.

Gettleman, Marvin E., and David Mermelstein, eds. *The Great Society Reader: The Failure of American Liberalism*. New York: Random House, 1967.

Ginger, Ray. *Age of Excess: The United States from 1877 to 1914*. New York: Macmillan, 1975.

Glazer, Nathan. "The Limits of Social Policy." *Commentary*, September 1971.

Goldman, Eric F. *The Tragedy of Lyndon Johnson*. New York: Knopf, 1969.

Graham, Hugh Davis. *The Uncertain Triumph: Federal Education Policy in the Kennedy and Johnson Years*. Chapel Hill: N.C. University of North Carolina Press, 1984.

Graubard, Stephen R. "Alarmist Critics Who Cry Beowulf." *New York Times*, October 1, 1987.

————. "Education Secretary Bennett Misperceives the Problems of American Higher Education." *Chronicle of Higher Education*, March 16, 1988.

Gross, Beatrice, and Ronald Gross, eds. *The Great School Debate*. New York: Simon and Schuster, 1985

Halperin, Samuel. "ESEA: The Positive Side." *Phi Delta Kappan*, November 1975.

Harrington, Michael. *The Other America: Poverty in the United States*. New York: Macmillan, 1962.

———. *The New American Poverty*. New York: Holt, Rinehart and Winston, 1984.

———. *The Long-Distance Runner*. New York: Holt, 1988.

Henderson, John C. *Thomas Jefferson: Views on Education*. New York: AMS Press, 1970.

Hofstader, Richard, and Wilson Smith, eds. *American Higher Education: A Documentary History*. Vol. 1. Chicago: University of Chicago Press, 1961.

Howard, M. William. "How the School Prayer Amendment Attacks Religious Liberty." *Education Digest*, December 1982.

Howe, Harold II. "Oral History Interview." Austin, Tex.: Lyndon B. Johnson Presidential Library, July 12, 1968.

Hunt, Gaillard. *The Writings of James Madison*. Vol. 9. New York: Doubleday, 1910.

Jefferson, Thomas. *The Writings of Thomas Jefferson*. Vol. 8. Washington, D.C.: Taylor and Maury, 1856.

Jeffrey, Julie Roy. *Education for the Children of the Poor*. Columbus: Ohio State University Press, 1978.

Johnson, Lyndon B. "State of the Union Message." *New York Times*, January 9, 1964.

———. "Acceptance Speech—Democratic Party Convention." *New York Times*, August 28, 1964.

———. "Education Message." *New York Times*, January 13, 1965.

———. "Inaugural Address." *New York Times*, January 21, 1965.

———. "State of the Union Message." *New York Times*, January 18, 1966.

———. "State of the Union Message." *New York Times*, January 11, 1967.

———. "State of the Union Message." *New York Times*, January 18, 1968.

———. *The Vantage Point: Perspectives on the Presidency, 1963-1969*. New York: Holt, Rinehart and Winston, 1971.

Judis, John B. "Mister ED." *New Republic*, April 27, 1987.

Kaplan, George. "Hail to a Chief or Two: The Indifferent Presidential Record in Education." *Phi Delta Kappan*, September 1984.

———. "New Beginnings, New Limits: Education and the 1988 Presidential Election." *Phi Delta Kappan*, October 1988.

Kearns, Doris. *Lyndon Johnson and the American Dream*. New York: Harper and Row, 1976.

Kennedy, Gail, ed. *Education for Democracy*. Boston: D.C. Heath, 1952.

Kennedy, John F. "Acceptance Speech—Democratic National Convention." *New York Times*, July 16, 1960.

———. "Inaugural Address." *New York Times*, January 21, 1961.

———. "State of the Union Message." *New York Times*, January 31, 1961.

———. "State of the Union Message." *New York Times*, January 12, 1962.

———. "State of the Union Message." *New York Times*, Western ed., January 15, 1963.

Kennedy, Paul. *The Rise and Fall of the Great Powers: Economic Change and Military Conflict from 1500 to 2000*. New York: Random House, 1987.

Keppel, Francis. "Oral History Interview." Austin, Tex.: Lyndon B. Johnson Presidential Library, April 21, 1969.

Kirkland, Edward C. *Industry Comes of Age: Business, Labor, and Public Policy 1860-1897*. New York: Holt, Rinehart and Winston, 1961.

Kizer, George A. "Federal Aid to Education 1945-1963." *History of Education Quarterly,* Spring 1970.

Landry, Marc, ed. *Modern Presidents and the Presidency.* Lexington, Mass.: Lexington Books, 1985.

Lane, David Marden. "The Cold War and American Education." Ann Arbor, Mich.: UMI Dissertations, 1957.

Lapati, Americo D. *Education and the Federal Government.* New York: Mason/ Charter, 1975.

Lazar, Irving, and Richard B. Darlingon. *Lasting Effects After Preschool.* Ithaca, N.Y.: Cornell University Press, 1978.

Levitan, Sar A., and Robert Taggart. *The Promise of Greatness.* Cambridge, Mass.: Harvard University Press, 1976.

Lewis, Anne C. "Looking for Leadership." *Phi Delta Kappan,* June 1989.

————. "A Box Full of Tools But No Blueprint." *Phi Delta Kappan,* November 1989.

Light, Paul Charles. *President's Agenda: Domestic Policy Choice from Kennedy to Carter.* Baltimore: Johns Hopkins University Press, 1982.

Link, Arthur S., ed. *The Papers of Woodrow Wilson.* Vol. 40. Princeton, N.J.: Princeton University Press, 1982.

Lodge, Henry Cabot, ed. *The Works of Alexander Hamilton.* Vol. 4. New York: G.P. Putnam and Sons, 1904.

McCoy, Charles Dean. *The Education President: Lyndon Baines Johnson's Public Statements on Instruction and the Teaching Profession.* Austin: University of Texas Press, 1975.

McCoy, Donald R. *The Presidency of Harry S. Truman.* Lawrence: University Press of Kansas, 1984.

MacDonald, Dwight. "Our Invisible Poor." *New Yorker,* January 19, 1963.

Madison, James. *Journal of the Federal Convention.* Freeport, N.Y.: Books for Libraries Press, 1970.

Mapp, Alf J., Jr. *Thomas Jefferson: A Strange Case of Mistaken Identity.* New York: Madison Books, 1987.

Moore, Donald R., and Suzanne Davenport. "School Choice: The New Improved Sorting Machine." National Invitational Conference on Public School Choice, Minneapolis, Minn., February 24, 1989.

Morgan, Ted. *FDR: A Biography.* New York: Simon and Schuster, 1985.

Morris, Aldon D. *The Origins of the Civil Rights Movement: Black Communities Organizing for Change.* New York: Free Press, 1984.

Moynihan, Daniel Patrick. *Maximum Feasible Misunderstanding.* New York: Free Press, 1969.

Murray, Charles. *Losing Ground: American Social Policy 1959-1980.* New York: Basic Books, 1984.

Myers, William Starr, ed. *The State Papers and Other Writings of Herbert Hoover.* Vol. 1. Garden City, N.Y.: Doubleday and Doran, 1934.

National Center for Educational Statistics. *Digest of Educational Statistics, 1989.* Washington, D.C.: U.S. Government Printing Office, 1989.

Neill, Shirley Boes. "The Reagan Education Record in California." *Phi Delta Kappan,* October 1989.

Nixon, Richard M. "Message on Education Reform." *American Education*, April 1970.

O'Hara, William T. *John F. Kennedy on Education*. New York: Teachers College Press, 1966.

Olson, Keith W. *The G.I. Bill, the Veterans and the Colleges*. Lexington: University Press of Kentucky, 1974.

Peterson, Merrill D., ed. *Thomas Jefferson: A Reference Biography*. New York: Charles Scribner's Sons, 1986.

Pipho, Chris. "Switching Labels: From Vouchers to Choice." *Education Week*, February 1, 1989.

Piven, Frances Fox, and Richard A. Cloward. *Poor People's Movements: Why They Succeed, How They Fail*. New York: Random House, 1977.

Provenzo, Eugene F., Jr. "Lincoln and Education." *Educational Studies*. Summer 1982.

Public Papers of the Presidents of the United States: Harry S. Truman. Washington, D.C.: U.S. Government Printing Office, 1965.

Ravitch, Diane. *The Troubled Crusade: American Education 1945-1980*. New York: Basic Books, 1983.

Ravitch, Diane, and Chester E. Finn, Jr. *What Do Our 17 Year Olds Know? A Report on the First National Assessment of History and Literature*. New York: Harper and Row, 1987.

Reagan, Ronald. *The Creative Society*. New York: Devin-Adair, 1968.

———. "School Prayer Amendment." *American Education*, July 1982.

———. "State of the Union Message—1983." *Vital Speeches of the Day*, February 15, 1983.

———. "The President's Address to the National Forum on Excellence in Education." *American Education*, March 1983.

———. "The President's Radio Address to the Nation on Education." *American Education*, May 1983.

———. "State of the Union: 1984." *New York Times*, January 26, 1984.

———. "State of the Union: 1985." *New York Times*, February 7, 1985.

———. "State of the Union: 1986." *New York Times*, February 5, 1986.

———. *Ronald Reagan's Weekly Radio Addresses: The President Speaks to America*. Vol. 1, *The First Term*. Compiled by Fred L. Israel. Wilmington, Del.: Scholarly Resources Inc., 1987.

———. "State of the Union: 1988." *New York Times*, January 26, 1988.

———. "Address to the Republican Party National Convention." *New York Times*, August 16, 1988.

———. "Remarks on the White House Workshop on Choice in Education." *Improving Schools and Empowering Parents: Choice in American Education*. Washington, D.C.: U.S. Government Printing Office, October 1989.

——— (with Richard G. Hubler). *Where's the Rest of Me?* New York: Karz, 1965.

Reedy, George. *Lyndon B. Johnson: A Memoir*. New York: Andrews and McNeel, 1982.

Reutter, E. Edmund, Jr., and Robert R. Hamilton, eds. *The Law of Public Education*. 2d ed. Mineola, N.Y.: Foundation Press, 1976.

Rickover, Hyman G. *Education and Freedom*. New York: E.P. Dutton, 1959.

The Rockefeller Panel. *Prospects for America*. Garden City, N.Y.: Doubleday, 1961.

Roosevelt, Franklin Delano. "Message to Congress." *New York Times,* November 24, 1943.

Rosenman, Samuel I., ed. *The Public Papers and Addresses of Franklin D. Roosevelt.* Vol. 11. New York: Russell and Russell, 1950.

Rudolph, Frederick, ed. *Essays on Education in the Early Republic.* Cambridge, Mass.: Harvard University Press, 1965.

Schlesinger, Arthur M., Jr. *A Thousand Days: John F. Kennedy and the White House.* Boston: Houghton Mifflin, 1965.

Shanker, Albert. "No Reason for Separate Education Department." *New York Times,* March 4, 1979.

———. "Nothing 'Voluntary' in School Prayer." *New York Times,* November 9, 1982.

———. "Competition and Choice: But Will Schools Improve?" *New York Times,* February 12, 1989.

———. "Peak or Pique?" *New York Times,* September 17, 1989.

———. "A Generous Vision." *New York Times,* October 8, 1989.

Shavelson, Richard J., and David C. Berliner. "Erosion of the Education Research Infrastructure." *Educational Research,* January-February 1988.

Sheehy, Gail. *Character: America's Search for Leadership.* New York: William Morrow, 1988.

Sidey, Hugh. "School Days, Then and Now." *Time,* July 11, 1983.

Smith, Martin. "Lessons from the California Experience." *Change,* September 1980.

Smith, Page. *The Rise of Industrial America: A People's History of the Post Reconstruction Era.* Vol. 6. New York: McGraw-Hill, 1984.

Spring, Joel. *The Sorting Machine Revisited: National Educational Policy Since 1945.* New York: Longman, 1989.

Starr, S. Frederick. Review of *Our Children and Our Country. Washington Post.* October 18, 1988.

"Statement by the President and Governor." *New York Times,* October 1, 1989.

Stickney, Benjamin D., and Lawrence R. Marcus. *The Great Education Debate: Washington and the Schools.* Springfield, Ill.: C.C. Thomas, 1984.

Teeter, Ruskin. *The Opening Up of American Education.* New York: University Press of America, 1983.

Thorpe, Francis Newton, ed. *The Statesmanship of Andrew Jackson: As Told in His Writings and Speeches.* New York: Tandy and Thomas, 1909.

Thurow, Lester C. *The Zero-Sum Society.* New York: Penguin Books, 1981.

Truman, Harry S. "State of the Union Message." *New York Times,* September 7, 1945.

———. "State of the Union Message." *New York Times,* January 6, 1946.

———. "State of the Union Message." *New York Times,* January 7, 1947.

———. *Years of Trial and Hope 1946-1952.* Garden City, N.Y.: Doubleday, 1956.

U.S. Bureau of the Census. *Historical Statistics of the United States: Colonial Times to 1970.* 2 vols. Washington, D.C.: U.S. Government Printing Office, 1975.

U.S. Department of Commerce. *Statistical Abstract of the United States.* Washington, D.C.: U.S. Government Printing Office, 1989.

U.S. Department of Education. *A Nation at Risk: The Imperative for Educational Reform.* Washington D.C.: Government Printing Office, 1983.

————. *Improving Schools and Empowering Parents: Choice in American Education.* Washington, D.C.: U.S. Government Printing Office, 1983.

————. *Japanese Education Today.* Washington, D.C.: U.S. Government Printing Office, 1987.

Verstegen, Deborah A., and David L. Clark. "The Diminution in Federal Expenditures for Education During the Reagan Administration." *Phi Delta Kappan,* October 1988.

Wall, James M. "A Troubled Nation May Consider Prayer." *The Christian Century,* June 2, 1982.

Wayson, William W. et al. *Up from Excellence: The Impact of the Excellence Movement on the Schools.* Bloomington, Ind.: Phi Delta Kappa Foundation, 1988.

Weikart, David P. et al. *Changed Lives: The Effects of the Perry Preschool Program on Youth Through Age 19.* Ypsilanti, Mich.: High Scope Press, 1984.

Wicker, Tom. "Bush's Report Card." *New York Times,* October 6, 1989.

Wilson, Robin. "Education Department Official in Charge of Research Thrives on Controversy While Seeking to Bolster Field." *Chronicle of Higher Education,* November 23, 1987.

Wilson, Woodrow. "What is a College For?" *Scribner's Magazine,* November 1909.

Index

About the Author

MAURICE R. BERUBE is Professor of Education at Old Dominion University. He is the author of *Teacher Politics: The Influence of Unions* (Greenwood Press, 1988), *Education and Poverty: Effective Schooling in the United States and Cuba* (Greenwood Press, 1984) and *The Urban University in America* (Greenwood Press, 1978); coauthor of *School Boards and School Policy* (Praeger, 1973) and *Local Control in Education* (Praeger, 1972); and coeditor of *Confrontation at Ocean Hill-Brownsville* (Praeger, 1969). His articles have been published in *The Urban Review, Commonweal, The Nation, Social Policy, New Politics, Cross Currents* and other journals.